it all depends

it all depends

A PRAGMATIC APPROACH TO ORGANIZATION

BY
HARVEY SHERMAN
Director, Organization and Procedures Department
The Port of New York Authority

UNIVERSITY OF ALABAMA PRESS
University, Alabama

HD
31
S45

Dedicated to Evelyn, Danny, and Josh.

contents

preface

This book is based on a series of five lectures given at the University of Alabama in the fall of 1962 under the auspices of the Southern Regional Training Program in Public Administration, and under the title, "Organizing to Determine and Achieve Agency Objectives".

The change in title from that used for the lectures to that used for the book results primarily from the fact that nobody liked the earlier title. Also, the new title tells the prospective reader a bit more accurately what the book is about.

The long interval between delivery of the lectures and publication of the book is attributable solely to procrastination on my part. Whether this delay means that practitioners are in fact, as they claim to be, too busy to write, or that practitioners find it difficult and uncomfortable to write, or that the slogan "publish or perish" is irrelevant to practitioners, or is the result of deeper and more personal psychological factors will have to remain unanswered unless and until some enterprising young behavioral scientist, with nothing better to do, decides that uncovering the answers would make a good research project.

I want to make it very clear at the outset that I have tried to present in this book, as in the lectures, some of the things I have learned *as a practitioner*, though I have undoubtedly also been influenced by the relevant literature. I have not tried to formulate a new and grandiose "general theory of organization". I have not tried to devise a new terminology to describe organizational phenomena. Such attempts are plentiful in the literature, for those who desire them. Nor have I tried to give the student what his professors are giving him—certainly much more effectively than I could. This book is for practitioners and practitioners-to-be. It is not for professors or professors-to-be, who will undoubtedly find it somewhat old-fashioned, or even quaint in this modern world of mathematical formulae, digital computers, quantitative analysis, cybernetics, and synectics.

I am indebted to many people for many useful suggestions. Where I agreed with a suggestion, I have tried to incorporate it in the manuscript, though perhaps not to the full satisfaction of the suggestor. Where I disagreed, or where I agreed but didn't quite know how to cope with the point raised, or where to have accepted the suggestion would have meant writing a different book—I have tried to forget that the suggestion was made.

My special thanks go to the following people: For reading and contributing valuable comments on the entire manuscript, to my colleagues at The Port of New York Authority, Daniel Kurshan, Elwood Holstein, Bernard Schein, and Philip Kelly; to my colleagues on the Organization Development Council, Charles Dexter of the New York Life Insurance Co., Hugh Estes of the General Electric Co., Denis Philipps of New York University, and Harold Stieglitz of the National Industrial Conference Board; and to Professor Herbert Kaufman of Yale University. Special thanks go also to my colleagues in the Port Authority, Leslie Edie and Wesley Hurley, for reading Chapter Five and making useful suggestions for its improvement.

I want also to thank Professors Robert B. Highsaw and Coleman B. Ransone, Jr. of the University of Alabama for asking me to deliver the lectures, for their many personal courtesies while I was at the University, and for their "gentle" reminders, in later months, that I had a manuscript to complete.

I must also express my gratitude to the book and magazine publishers, and individual authors of unpublished works, who have granted permission to quote from various publications, as indicated in the Notes. Particular acknowledgment is due those who authorized fairly lengthy quotations or paraphrases as follows: Inter-University Case Program for permission to quote from *The New York City Health Centers* by Herbert Kaufman, published by Bobbs-Merrill Publishing Co., copyright 1959; Richard D. Irwin, Inc. for permission to paraphrase from *Man and Organization: Three Problems in Human Relations in Industry* by William Foote Whyte, copyright 1959; McGraw-Hill, Inc., for permission to quote from *New Patterns of Management* by Rensis Likert, copyright 1961; *Engineering and Science Monthly*, published at the California Institute of Technology, for permission to quote from "A Case Study in Innovation" by Elting E. Morison, copyright 1950; the *Harvard Business Review* for permission to quote from "Innovation Challenges Conformity" by John J. Corson, copyright 1962; "Unhuman Organizations" by Harold J. Leavitt, copyright 1962; and "Information Technology and Decentralization" by John F. Burlingame, copyright 1961; the *Journal of Politics* for permission to quote from "The Politics of Administrative Organization: A Case History" by Francis E. Rourke, copyright 1957; and the *Public Administration Review* for permission to quote from "Do Federal Managers Manage?" by John E. Fisher, copyright 1962; "The Network of Authority" by O. Glenn Stahl, copyright 1958; and "Birth of an Organization: The Economic Cooperation Administration" by Herbert A. Simon, copyright 1953. My thanks to Sherman Kingsbury for permission to quote from his unpublished paper, "Arthur D. Little, Inc., A Small Society"; to Frederick C. Mosher for permission to paraphrase some of his comments made in a panel session at the 1962 annual conference of the American Political Science Association; and to W. H. Nesbitt for permission to use a classification of types of delegation developed by him.

I am not sure how many, if any, readers of a book actually

look at the Preface. Indeed, I'm not sure why anyone should. But to those who may read the Preface of *this* book, let me say that I hope that they enjoy reading the book as much as I enjoyed delivering the lectures and preparing the manuscript. Naturally, I also hope that they will find the book to be of some use.

Harvey Sherman

April 1966

it all depends

premises and patterns

Many an experienced, practical, hard–headed and successful executive, whether in government or business, has been heard to say that good people will make any kind of organization work successfully—that it doesn't really matter how an agency (or a company) is organized. Other executives, equally experienced, equally practical, equally hard–headed, and equally successful, say that there are only two (or three, or four) basic rules of organization, such as "No one should have more than one boss", or "Authority should be commensurate with responsibility", or, perhaps, "Related functions should be grouped together", and so on.

Specialists in organization planning, whether they be practitioners or students, would ordinarily not be quite so categorical. Being specialists, their self–interest in their own field would prevent them from taking the first view. But also, being specialists, they are too aware of how much they don't know to take the second. Nevertheless, specialists also tend to cluster around two core positions: that people constitute the essential ingredient in organization, or conversely that there are universal, or nearly universal, principles of organization that can be determined independent of particular people.*

* Harry Golden has said that there are two kinds of people in the world: those who insist on dividing the world into two kinds of people, and those

Where does truth lie? Will good people make any organization work well? Are there universal rules of organization independent of people? Does truth lie somewhere in between? What is organization, anyway, and does the type of organizational pattern make any real difference? If so, to whom and for what? Or possibly, do we yet know enough to answer these questions? It is my hope that those with patience enough to stick with me until the end will be in a better position to answer such questions for themselves.

A TYPICAL PROBLEM OF ORGANIZATION

It might be well to set the stage with an example of a specific organization problem. Back in 1949, as a result of a recession, Sears, Roebuck & Company made a study of how its intermediate size department stores were organized.[1] These stores ordinarily had 32 departments. No instructions or guidance as to their organizational structure had been given by headquarters. In the course of the study, it was found that two common patterns had developed. One, referred to as Type X, had a manager, an assistant manager, and 32 department heads reporting directly to them. (See Fig. 1)

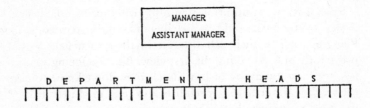

FIGURE 1. TYPE "X" STORES

The other, referred to as Type Y, had a manager, five or six

who don't. Based on the way I have started out, I would appear to be one of the former.

assistant managers, and four to six department heads reporting to each assistant manager. (See Fig. 2)

When the effectiveness of these two types of stores was compared in terms of profits, costs, and number of management personnel considered promotable to higher levels, the Type X stores proved to be superior on all three counts. This conclusion comes as a shock to most executives who have been conditioned to believe that a small span of control is the first "law" of organization.

Why did Type X work better for Sears? Essentially because the manager and assistant manager, not being able to supervise all their department heads closely, had to select persons with initiative, good judgment, and the ability to take responsibility and then let them pretty much alone except for holding them accountable for results.

Further analysis revealed that the managers of Type X stores tended to be "optimists" about people. They believed that most people want to do a good job and they had faith in their subordinates. Managers of Type Y stores tended to be "pessimists" about people. They believed that by-and-large people don't want to work, that "the modern generation has gone to pot", etc.[2] As a result, managers of X–type stores, when put in

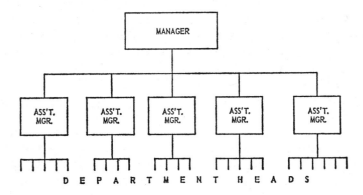

FIGURE 2. TYPE "Y" STORES

charge of stores organized on the Y basis, soon found that they
didn't need the extra layer of supervision and could save money
by eliminating it. Managers of Y–type stores, on the other hand,
put in charge of stores organized on the X basis, soon found
that they could not supervise so many people directly and felt
the need to establish a new level of supervision to help manage
the numerous departments.

Am I trying to show through this case that a large span of
control is necessarily better than a small span of control? Definitely not. What I think this case does demonstrate is that:

1.   The way an enterprise is organized can make a difference.

2.   The pattern of organization does have some relationship
to people (in this case, at least to the personality of the manager).

3.   "Doing what comes naturally" (e.g., optimists organizing
with a large span of control) can be more effective than following the text book rule.

4.   For Sears Roebuck & Company, in 1949, for intermediate
size stores, with optimist-type managers, a large span of control worked better than a small span of control, when measured
by profits, costs, and development of people. It is undoubtedly
true, of course, that under certain other circumstances a small
span of control would be more effective. My point here is
simply that the most effective organization depends upon the
situation. I shall say more about this later.

WHAT THIS BOOK IS ABOUT

Having, I hope, aroused the reader's interest in the subject
of organization, I would like now to go back and outline briefly
what I plan to cover in this and subsequent chapters. Perhaps
I can best start by stating what I plan *not* to do.

This book is not designed as a "how to" guide for the specialist in organization planning. Therefore I will not go into

methods of research and analysis used in studying a problem of organization or into the specialized tools of the organization planner such as the organization manual, the functional organization chart, the linear responsibility chart, or the job description.

This book is not designed to set forth any new way of thinking about organization in terms of the authority structure, bureaucracy, sociological relationships, or mathematical formulae. I will also stay away from any detailed review of the behavior of people in small face-to-face groups, or what is usually referred to as group dynamics or interpersonal relationships. I don't have any easy or final answers to organization problems. And I have no pet theory of organization to sell, unless it is pragmatism, and many people object to calling that a theory.

Rather, my aim is at the person who is either now a practicing manager in government or industry, or who is a student planning to become a practicing manager. For such people, my purpose is to arouse in them an interest in the problem of organizing, to make them aware of the importance of the subject, to bring to their attention some of the major current and likely future problems in this field, and to provide a general framework for thinking about the subject.

In the rest of this chapter, I plan to identify some of my own biases, to define the process of organizing, to compare the problem of organization in government and in industry, to discuss why the subject of organization is important and apt to become more important, to review some of the major reasons for the prevalence of poor organization structure, to touch on the question of where responsibility for organization planning lies, and to sketch the different basic patterns of organizational structure and the advantages and disadvantages of each.

In Chapter Two, I will review the value and limitations of the so–called principles of organization, propose a pragmatic approach to organizing, and discuss the importance of perspective. In Chapter Three, I will deal with some of the basic

problems of organization such as staff–line relationships, decentralization, delegation, and effecting organizational changes.
In Chapter Four, I will cover some of the principal pitfalls and
platitudes in organizing. And in the final chapter I will analyze
some of the major social and technological factors that affect
organization, and take a look at what the future may bring.

SOME PERSONAL PREMISES, ASSUMPTIONS, AND BIASES

I suppose that it would be desirable at this point to identify,
insofar as I can, my major premises, assumptions, and biases.
They will undoubtedly show up throughout the book. Among
them certainly are the following:

That organizing is still more an art than a science—an art in
which thinking is more important than doctrine, common
sense more important than expertise.

That the most effective overall approach to problems of organization is that of pragmatism (i.e., doing what "works" in a
particular situation, with due regard for both short and long
range objectives, rather than following any allegedly universal
rules).[3]

That one's perception of the "best" organization depends in
large part on the particular segment of the organization one
serves most directly.

That "flexibility" has become a more important word in organization than "equilibrium".

That "power and personalities" are more important in reaching organizational decisions than "efficiency and economy".

That the two most pervasive characteristics of the problem
of organization are complexity (what's "true" in one case is
often not "true" in another) and dynamics (what's "true" today
is not "true" tomorrow).

And that there is no one "ideal" or "best" organization except for a particular agency, at a particular time, with particu-

lar people, and that even then the best organization can only be best for some purposes and some people, while at the same time being less than the best for other purposes and other people.

If there is a dominant theme in my thinking about organization, it is illustrated by the following story. When I was working in the U.S. technical assistance program, an Israeli official came to the United States for a year's training in public administration. After traveling throughout the country for a good part of the year, he returned to Washington, D. C. for a "debriefing" session before going back to Israel. When asked what he had learned from his travels and observations, he replied, "You know, it's a funny thing. Wherever I went, whomever I saw, and whatever I asked, I always got the same answer. And that answer always consisted of the same three words. These words were: 'It all depends.' "[4] If there is any one "secret" behind successful management in the United States, and many foreign visitors seem to think that there is, in my judgment it lies in the pragmatic attitude expressed by those three words.

What Is Organization?

There are almost as many definitions of "organization" as there have been writers on the subject.[5] Early writers in the field of management tended to stress formal organizational structure and its use as a tool for achieving coordination and control. More recently, the emphasis has changed toward regarding organization as a social system with attention to informal as well as formal relationships among members of the organization. Most definitions, however, regardless of where the emphasis is placed, see organization as consisting of some five elements: grouping of activities, accomplishment of objectives, structure for coordination and control, people, and relationship among people and groups of people.

I find it much simpler to define "organizing" than "organization," since in this way I avoid the often–used meaning of "organization" as synonymous with the enterprise, the company, or the agency. And I prefer the word "organizing" to the frequently used expression "organization planning" because the latter term would seem to omit essential parts of the process, i.e., implementation and evaluation of organization plans.

I define "organizing" as the process of grouping activities and responsibilities, and establishing relationships (formal and informal), that will enable people to work together most effectively in determining and accomplishing the objectives of an enterprise.[6] Thus, the noun "organization" comes to mean either the product of the process of organizing, or the subject under discussion as I have defined it above. Note again that what I am talking about is something less than "organization" in the sense of a total institution or enterprise in all its aspects.[7] Of course, one could not "organize" effectively without taking into account these other aspects.

I believe that my definition is fairly close to most standard definitions except for the words "determining and", which are usually left out. Most writers apparently assume that objectives are "given", say by a legislature or a board of directors, and that the executive does no more than organize to carry out such objectives.

While certain objectives are almost always "given" from outside or "on high", the manager must always become involved in determining objectives either by (1) setting sub–objectives within overall objectives, or (2) developing recommendations for new or revised objectives to be considered by the legislative or other policy–making body.

A more simple working definition of organizing than the one I have given, but easier to keep in mind and adequate for most purposes, is that organizing is "dividing up the work".[8] The definition is simple; the process is not.

ORGANIZATION IN GOVERNMENT AND BUSINESS

Throughout this book I will make frequent reference to illustrations from the business world as well as from government. One very practical reason is simply that a large proportion of the research in the field of organization has taken place in a business setting. By comparison, relatively little such research has been published on the organization of specific government agencies.

There is a second reason, perhaps not so obvious on its face. This is that, in my judgment, the difference between government and business, between public and private enterprise, has been grossly exaggerated, at least insofar as organizational consequences to particular governmental agencies or private companies are concerned.[9]

It is generally agreed that the objectives of an enterprise significantly affect the organization of that enterprise. How different, then, are the objectives of government agencies and private business? Let's take a few examples.

1. The principal objective of a private airline (such as those in the United States) might be defined as follows: "To carry passengers and goods by air safely, speedily, courteously, and with a reasonable profit". The principal objective of a publicly owned airline (as many in Europe) might be: "To carry passengers and goods by air safely, speedily, courteously, with minimum cost to the taxpayer".

2. The principal objectives of a private university might be stated to be: "To educate our youth, to conduct research, and to push forward the frontiers of knowledge, to the extent possible with the funds available". I can't think of a better way of stating the objectives of a state university.

3. The principal objective of a private printing firm might be to print a high quality product at a reasonable profit. The principal objective of the Government Printing Office might be to print a high quality product as efficiently and economically as possible.

4. The principal objective of a private personnel office might be to recruit, develop, and retain the best possible employees—an objective identical to that of many public personnel offices.

Such examples could be multiplied many times—for both public and private hospitals, welfare agencies, utilities, and agencies engaged in scientific research, among others.

It is true that in many cases there is a difference—that of profit *vs.* non-profit. (When stated as profit *vs.* efficiency, the distinction loses some of its edge.) But even this is no universal test. Thus, some insurance companies operate under a profit motive, others are mutual companies and therefore non–profit. Both are non–governmental. Moreover, the insurance program of the Veterans Administration undoubtedly is much more like, than it is unlike, the programs of the non–governmental insurance companies.

Another way of stating the difference is in terms of private profit *vs.* the public interest. There is merit in this distinction. Nevertheless, more and more sophisticated observers of the business scene talk about the public–interest responsibilities of business; about the professional manager's responsibilities not only to the stockholders (for profit) but also to employees, suppliers, customers, the community, the general public.

The administrative cynic, *a la* Parkinson, might say that the principal objective of both government and industry is to increase in size. This is already a cliché about government, but there is evidence that at least some top business executives regard increasing total sales (an indicator of size) as more important than increasing net profits. And as for business executives below the top level, I am skeptical that the profit motive has any significant effect on either their mode of operation or their motivation.[10]

Far more meaningful to the organization planner are the specific differences in objectives among or between different enterprises, whether they be government agencies, private companies, or a mixture of both. Thus, for example, it would be crucial for the organizer to know that as between two civil service commissions (both governmental), the objectives of one were concerned only with "keeping the rascals out", whereas the objectives of the other also included those associated with modern so-called positive personnel administration. Similarly, as between two manufacturing companies (both private), it would be crucial to know that the objectives of one included the desire to expand into the international market, whereas the objectives of the other were to remain small and domestic, with high quality and low quantity production.

Further evidence of similarities between government and industry in a related field of management is furnished by Robert L. Kahn, Program Director of the Survey Research Center at the University of Michigan. Mr. Kahn points out that while most of the Center's studies of organizational behavior have been made in private industry, a number of them have been made in government agencies. He goes on to say: "It is our experience that the broad principles of leadership which have developed in our industrial work are on the whole applicable to the government agencies".[11]

After all, management, whether in government or business, is concerned with the same basic tasks—deciding what to do and getting it done effectively and efficiently. Of course, objectives will differ for different enterprises. But it is more helpful to analyze these objectives on an agency-by-agency, or company-by-company, or agency-by-company basis than it is to try to arrive at some overall "touchstone" that will distinguish between the objectives of government and business for all time (even assuming that it were possible to tell where government leaves off and private business begins under today's complex contractual arrangements between them).[12]

If we go beyond objectives to operations, as Austin J. Tobin has noted, ". . . it is difficult to think of any business task or occupation that cannot be found in government, just as it is difficult to think of any activity in the executive branch of the government that cannot be found in business". And he goes on to note that:

Government is beginning to look more like business. Government agencies are bargaining and dealing with employee organizations in a manner resembling labor–management relations in business. Revenue–producing government agencies are being established as public corporations, or authorities, or with corporate–type budgets that pinpoint accountability for net revenue results. Even among non–revenue agencies, performance standards and performance–type budgets focus legislative and public review on results measured in the business vernacular. Business machines look and work the same whether in a public or private organization, and modern government is as dependent upon such machines as modern business. The press and civic organizations are demanding ever higher standards of public service and are prodding government officials toward more satisfactory levels of performance. When the prodding fails they cry out for an aroused citizenry to demand corrective action.[13]

Is Organization Important?

The relationship between the way an enterprise is organized and the achievement of desired results is well demonstrated by the Sears Roebuck case already discussed. Additional evidence as to the importance of proper organization to the success of an enterprise is found in a recent survey made by *Dun's Review* of its Presidents Panel, which consists of the presidents of 171 of the largest U.S. corporations. The panel members were asked what factors they considered most crucial to future company success. Organizational planning tied for second place with research and development behind marketing strategy, but well ahead of production techniques, financial management, personnel management, labor relations and public relations.[14]

I know of no similar survey in the public field. However, the amount of heat engendered over many of the reorganization plans submitted by recent Presidents for congressional ratification, plus the amount of attention paid to the subject in both Hoover Commission reports and most of the so–called "Little Hoover Commission" reports would indicate that the problem is considered of some importance by public officials as well as private.

The problem of organizing is important to every manager since he must inevitably become involved in how the work of those whom he supervises is divided. There are many reasons to believe that the subject is apt to become more rather than less important. Let me mention just four:

1. As both government and business become bigger and more complex, the problem of organization becomes correspondingly more complex and more crucial to results.

2. The rapidity of technological change (automation, electronic data processing, and the like) since World War II, as compared with all of history before that time, is so much greater that the problem of organizing may well have changed in nature from one of adjusting organizations to meet present conditions (maintaining "equilibrium") to one of adjusting organizations to meet future (possibly yet unknown) conditions (maintaining desired "dis-equilibrium").

3. Rapidly increasing knowledge from the behavioral sciences about human relations and human behavior demonstrates that organizing is far more complex than a mechanical or engineering problem of structure. The task of organizing must also take into account the constantly shifting dynamics of interpersonal relations and the informal power structure.

4. The change in the proportion of blue-collar, relatively low-educated persons in the work force, toward more white-collar, higher educated persons results in a work force that is more concerned with how the organization affects individuals, and requiring more complicated methods of motivation.

These and related developments, and how they may affect organization, are discussed in greater detail in Chapter Five.

WHY ORGANIZATION GOES WRONG

Management consultants, whether working in industry or government, frequently find that organization is one of the major problems at the root of poor performance. A long list of reasons for this condition can be compiled—too numerous to cover here. The most important of these reasons appear to be as follows:

1. Inertia or social lag. Programs, key people, or other conditions have changed but organization has not kept up.

2. Failure to recognize that there is an organization problem. This might be due either to the fact that the agency or company is getting acceptable results despite poor organization (as in good economic times in industry), or that a problem is perceived but is regarded as other than organization (as poor morale) without recognition that this problem may itself be due in part to faulty organization.

3. Overemphasis on organization structure (the mechanics of organization rather than the dynamics) resulting in moving boxes around with no relationship to basic problems of decision–making, program emphasis, or utilization of people.

4. Copying the other fellow's chart. (What's good enough for General Electric, or DuPont, or General Motors, is good enough for me.)

5. Lack of willingness on the part of a top executive to make a needed organizational change because it will hurt a loyal, long–service subordinate.

6. Conversely, organizational actions taken by a top executive to solve a personality problem, without adequate regard for the other consequences of such decisions, or for other more appropriate solutions to the problem.

7. Inadequacies in organization theory. As we shall see in Chapter Two, the theorists have given us many "principles", but these principles frequently contradict each other and organization theory has not told us under what conditions each applies.

WHO IS RESPONSIBLE FOR EFFECTIVE ORGANIZATION?

Good management theory has it that every manager, whether he be the president or foreman in a private company, or the agency head or first-line supervisor in a government agency, is responsible for the effective organization of the units or people reporting to him.

In The Port of New York Authority we feel that this problem of responsibility for effective organization is so important that we have spelled it out in clear terms in the section of our Administrative Manual dealing with "The Organization of the Port Authority" as follows:

> Every supervisor, including the Executive Director as well as a first-line supervisor, is responsible for achieving the most effective organization of the work of the people whom he supervises. He is also responsible for obtaining professional staff advice on such matters whenever appropriate. If such advice is available and he does not seek it out, he has failed in his responsibility.
>
> . . . .
>
> Organization planning is the job of every supervisor. Specialized staff assistance and advice are available in this field, both from the Organization and Procedures Department and from outside management consulting firms, but all supervisors, at every level, are encouraged to:
>
> Become thoroughly familiar with Port Authority management principles affecting organization;
>
> Develop their own ideas as to the organization and functions of the groups whom they supervise and take the initiative for getting those ideas accepted and carried into effect;
>
> Plan their future organization pattern: anticipate forthcoming changes in personnel, programs, methods or responsibilities; foresee the organizational implications of these changes; and have an organization plan ready or in mind, for use when the right time arrives.[15]

It should be recognized, however, that there are instances where this "ideal" of clear-cut responsibility cannot be met fully. At the foreman level in industry, for example, the division of work is principally determined by procedures developed by industrial engineers.[16] The foreman may modify these procedures to a certain extent through informal methods, but they are often largely out of his control.

To take another example, the organization of many governmental agencies is set by legislation and is not subject to major changes by the agency head. Line item budgets and manning tables are other methods used in government that may limit the extent of changes in the division of work available to government executives. Legislating organization in any detail undoubtedly provides a rigidity which is undesirable from the point of view of efficiency and economy and is therefore almost unanimously opposed by experts in administration. Nevertheless, I think it can be assumed that there are political values to the legislators in legislating organization or they would not spend their time and energy on such problems.

Furthermore, in a large agency or company the problem of organization is so complex, and the time of the chief executive so much in demand, that he frequently will rely on specialists in organizational planning, whether they be on his staff or outside consultants, to assist in developing plans for changes in organization. In such cases, classical management theory would hold that the line manager is responsible for organizational decisions, while the staff organizational planner only advises. As we shall see in Chapter Three, this is an oversimplification. If the line manager makes bad organizational decisions, he will have to suffer the consequences. But it is equally true that if the staff organizational planner gives bad advice, he will also have to suffer the consequences. Thus, it seems to me that in fact there is a shared responsibility and accountability by both line and staff.

ALTERNATIVE PATTERNS OF ORGANIZATION

The final subject that I would like to cover in this chapter is that of the major alternative patterns available for grouping activities, and the advantages and disadvantages of each.[17] In

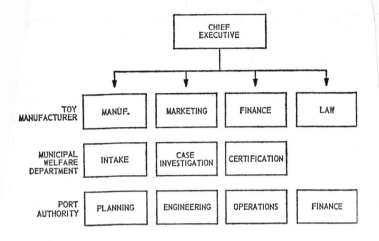

FIGURE 4. PROCESS OR FUNCTION ORGANIZATION

design bridges, tunnels, marine terminals, airports and land terminals; to supervise the construction of bridges, tunnels, marine terminals, airports and land terminals; and to inspect and test the materials going into the construction of bridges, tunnels, marine terminals, airports and land terminals.

On a process or function basis, the department would be organized as shown in Figure 5.

On a purpose or product basis, the organization pattern might appear as in Figure 6.

Note that the significant difference is where you put the supervisors.

I would like to point out that in each case I have been describing the organization pattern used only for the first level below the top man (whether agency head or department director). The next level might be organized along different lines. Thus, the toy manufacturing company organized on a product basis (dolls, blocks, sports equipment, games) on the first level, might well be organized on a process basis (manufacturing, marketing, etc.) at the next level of each product division.

practice, most enterprises will be orga⸺
tion of these ways. For purposes of anal⸺
ful to examine these alternatives in their

There are two basic ways of organizin⸺
"purpose" or "product", the other as "pro⸺

The purpose or product type of organizati⸺
all of the activities and work procedures ne⸺
plish a given purpose, or to produce and mar⸺
uct, are grouped together under the supervision⸺
Figure 3 shows how this might look for three⸺
of enterprises: a toy manufacturer, a municipa⸺
partment, and The Port of New York Authority.

The process or function type of organization, o⸺
hand, is one in which activities are grouped and su⸺
the basis of specialized technical skills, as shown in⸺

These two patterns of organization are usually als⸺
tive choices at lower levels than the agency or compa⸺
level. To take the engineering department of the Port ⸺
ity, for example, its functions (simplified) are as follo⸺

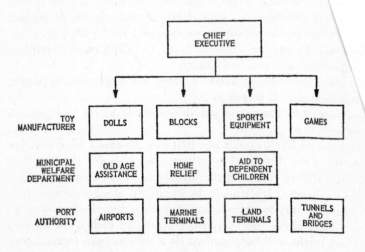

FIGURE 3. PURPOSE OR PRODUCT ORGANIZATION

This is not always the case, however. For example, the dolls division could well be further broken down on a sub–product

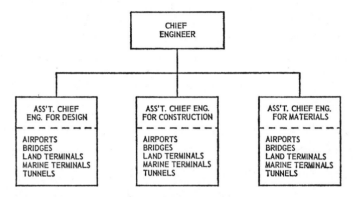

FIGURE 5. PROCESS OR FUNCTION ORGANIZATION OF ENGINEERING DEPARTMENT

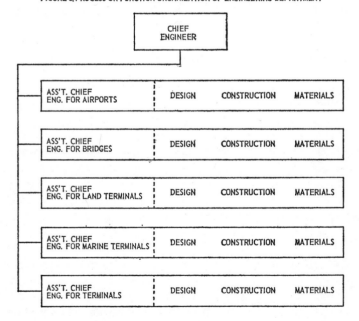

FIGURE 6. PURPOSE OR PRODUCT ORGANIZATION OF ENGINEERING DEPARTMENT

basis (rag dolls, china dolls) before being organized into process sub–units.

The trend in both industry and government has been to change from process or function to purpose or product.[18] The principal reason is growth in size, for the product or purpose type organization makes it possible to fix responsibility more clearly below the top executive for profit in business, or for accomplishing a particular purpose in government. This relieves the burden on the top man in a large enterprise. A second advantage, also helpful to the top man, is that coordination is easier, since there tends to be less conflict between product or purpose divisions than between process or function divisions. For example, a common problem in industry when profits decline under the functional type of organization is for the sales people to complain that no one could sell the poor-quality product being turned out by the manufacturing people, whereas the latter maintain that the product is fine but the salesmen are incompetent. Such conflicts are less apt to reach the chief executive under the product type organization, though a vice–president for a product division that is losing money will face the same problem among those reporting to him.

Other advantages of the product or purpose type organization are: (1) the second level executives get broader experience and therefore, other things being equal, should be better qualified for promotion than specialists in particular processes or functions; (2) employees will tend to be more able to see the end product and how their own work fits into it; (3) the danger that the processes may come to be regarded as ends in themselves, rather than as means, is reduced.

These are powerful advantages, and one might well wonder why an enterprise would be organized any other way. However, the process or function pattern does have its virtues. For one thing, it allows for the more economical utilization of technical skills, machines, and equipment. To take a simple example, under the process type of organization, one set of accounting machines might well serve the entire enterprise, whereas a complete product or purpose breakdown would require a separate set of accounting machines for each division.

Other advantages of the process type of organization are that it promotes quality in technical decision, since all those with the same technical skill are in one group; it fosters professional development by association of people with like training and knowledge and makes it easier to establish separate junior, intermediate, and senior levels for advancement; it may cancel out fluctuations in workload; it makes for more consistency in technical decisions; and under certain circumstances it may reduce undue influence by outsiders. In addition, the process type organization frequently promotes loyalty to the objectives of the enterprise as a whole, whereas the product or purpose type often leads to loyalties for particular segments of the enterprise.

The disadvantages of each of these patterns of organization tend to be the opposites of the advantages of the other.[19] Thus, it is simply not possible to have all the advantages and none of the disadvantages of both patterns. This being so, the result in practice is nearly always a compromise. In a change from a process or functional organization to a product or purpose organization, adopted to achieve such advantages as fixing responsibility below the top and building broader-gauged executives, some activities will normally continue to be operated on a centralized basis (usually in "staff" units) to achieve economy and technical quality. It should be recognized, however, that this compromise reduces the "full" responsibility of the product or purpose head, and reduces the breadth of experience he gets.

There are two additional patterns of grouping activities, "area" and "clientele", which are basically variations of the product or purpose type, since one supervisor is responsible for all types of work in each.

The area pattern groups activities on the basis of the geographic area to be served, and might appear as in Figure 7.

The main advantage of organizing by area is that it tends

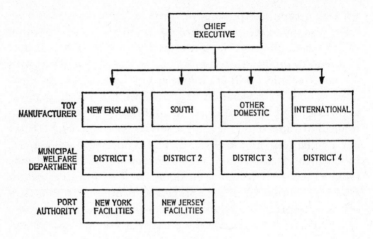

FIGURE 7. AREA ORGANIZATION

to lead to decisions more appropriate for a particular geographical area. The main disadvantages are that it is difficult to get consistency among areas and it may be overly expensive because of the need to duplicate staffs, equipment, and the like.

What I have said about area organization concerns the organization of the headquarters office. The problem of organizing as between a headquarters office on the one hand, and field offices or plants on the other, is a fascinating and complex problem in itself, and one that deserves more treatment than can be given in this book.

The clientele pattern groups activities on the basis of clientele groups being served, and might appear as in Figure 8.

The principal advantages of this type of organization are that it is easy to get consistent treatment of a particular clientele and, in some circumstances, makes it easier to maintain good public relations (since, for example, a client has one place in the organization to go for all his services). The principal disadvantages are that coordination is difficult, the divisions may become "advocates" of particular groups of clients, and it tends to be expensive due to duplicate staffs, equipment, etc.

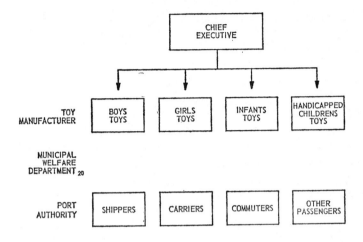

FIGURE 8. CLIENTELE ORGANIZATION

It is a mistake to think of any one of these patterns as being based on specialization while others are not. All are based on specialization—but specilization in different things. It is true that the type of specialization under the process or function pattern (sales, production, finance, engineering, law, etc.) is less like the job of the chief executive than specialization in product or purpose, area, or clientele, since each of these requires some knowledge of all the processes or functions.

I have already mentioned size as an important factor affecting the pattern of organization selected. Other important factors are:

1. Policies and program objectives of the enterprise.

2. Nature and amount of workload, including people and things dealt with and skills required.

3. Stability or changing nature of the enterprise (e.g., need for decisions to be made at the top in an organization where policies are not yet set).

4. Complexity of activities (e.g., number of products, geographic dispersion of operations).

5. Capacity of executives.

6. Available resources (money, materials, manpower).
7. Public relations and political implications.
8. Speed requirements.
9. Quality requirements.
10. Traditional patterns and informal requirements.

In Chapter One, I have covered some of my basic premises, a definition of "organizing", organization in government and industry, the importance of this subject, the major reasons why ineffective organization is found, responsibility for achieving and maintaining effective organization, and something about the alternative patterns of organization available. In Chapter Two, I will discuss the values and limitations of principles of organization, pragmatism as an approach to organization problems, and the importance of perspective in viewing the organization structure.

TWO

principles, pragmatism, and perspective

Two decades ago, in a brilliant article entitled "The Proverbs of Administration",[21] Professor Herbert A. Simon started a controversy that is still raging.

PRINCIPLES = PROVERBS

Professor Simon's thesis was that "principles" of administration, unfortunately (or fortunately, from the point of view of rationalizing past decisions), are like proverbs in that for each principle, as for each proverb, there is another that contradicts it. Compare, for instance, "Look before you leap" and "He who hesitates is lost". It makes a nice parlor game to think of other pairs: "Many heads are better than one" and "Too many cooks spoil the broth"; "Absence makes the heart grow fonder" and "Out of sight, out of mind"; "The meek shall inherit the earth" and "The Lord helps them who help themselves". It is extremely difficult to think of a proverb that is not contradicted by some other proverb, equally persuasive.

Perhaps the most obvious example of an analogous relationship in organization theory is evident in the contradictory principles that "The span of control (i.e., the number of people

reporting to one superior) should be limited"[22] *vs.* "The number of levels between the chief executive and the workers at
the bottom of the hierarchy should be kept to a minimum".
Given the same number of employees in an organization, it is
clear that if the span of control is small, the number of levels
must be large, and contrariwise, if the span of control is large,
the number of levels must be small.

The case made by Professor Simon seems compelling to me
—but not to everyone. For example, a recent article by John
E. Fisher criticizing federal managers[23] states:

> The basic rules-of-thumb of organization are so simple and
> obvious that it is particularly disturbing to see them disregarded.
> Among the most important but most troublesome rules are the
> following:
>   1. Each function should be assigned to only one organizational
>   unit.
>   2. Responsibility for a function should be matched by the au-
>   thority necessary to perform the function.
>   3. Authority to act should be as close as possible to the level at
>   which the work is performed.[24]

When we examine these "rules-of-thumb" closely they turn
out to be neither simple nor obvious. Of course, Mr. Fisher
cannot be accused of inventing these statements. They have
been repeated as basic principles of organizing in countless
textbooks, articles, and speeches; and they are accepted by
countless practitioners, in theory if not operationally.

ONE FUNCTION—ONE UNIT

Mr. Fisher's first rule is that each function should be assigned to only one organizational unit. This rule is plainly of
no help in telling us whether process type functions (e.g., accounting, law, etc.) should be grouped together, whether purpose or product type functions should be grouped together,

whether all functions dealing with the same geographic area should be grouped together, or whether all functions dealing with the same clientele should be grouped together. Thus, it is of no value in helping us decide which functions to group together in one organization unit; i.e., which of the various basic patterns of organization discussed in Chapter One should be adopted. How, for example, would this rule help an agency involved in providing technical assistance to underdeveloped countries to decide whether to organize by country or region on the one hand, or by type of technical assistance (e.g., agriculture, public health, education) on the other?

Moreover, this principle is simply invalid for many functions. For example, since every manager is involved in personnel work, it is not feasible to assign the entire personnel function to "only one organizational unit"—similarly with planning, budgeting, reporting and many other functions. As a matter of fact, two of the major issues in organization, staff–line relationships and centralization *vs.* decentralization (both of which are discussed in more detail in Chapter Three), are concerned with precisely this problem of how to divide a function among different organization units. The problem of staff–line relationships is concerned with how to divide a function between line and staff (as the personnel function), and the problem of centralization *vs.* decentralization is concerned with how to divide a function vertically between different levels, and therefore different units, of the enterprise.

It should also be noted that "assigning each function to only one organization unit" implies organization by type of work. There are, of course, many other valid ways of organizing; e.g., by the skills, interests, and talents of the supervisors involved; or by the friendships, social relationships, traditions, and customs of the employees involved. The actual organization will usually be a compromise between formal considerations (i.e., type of work) and informal considerations, as well as those I have just mentioned.

AUTHORITY AND RESPONSIBILITY

Mr. Fisher's second rule is that responsibility for a function
should be matched by the authority necessary to perform the
function. Here we begin with a semantic problem. The word
"authority" means different things to different "authorities".
There are at least four common meanings for this word in the
literature: (1) The formal authority conveyed by rank and
position to give orders to subordinates; (2) the authority of
the subordinate to obey, disobey, or partially obey the orders
of his superior; (3) the authority that is inherent in the job
itself, and (4) the authority of knowledge and persuasion.[25] Mr.
Fisher is not explicit about his definition of authority, but
seems to be using it in the first sense. Even though many executives exercise in informal ways authority that they may not
have in a formal sense, let's look at the proposition from the
point of view of formal authority.

Everyone who has worked in government is familiar with
the fact that agency heads are responsible for carrying out the
objectives of their agencies in the face of a multitude of limitations on their authority set by central staff agencies. Thus, for
example, central budget divisions may limit their freedom of
action by line item controls, controls over the establishment of
new positions, or by allotments and apportionments of funds;
central civil service commissions or personnel departments may
limit their authority by classifying positions in certain grades,
by limiting appointments to persons with "civil service status",
or by requiring specified education and experience for appointments and promotions; and central accounting units limit their
authority by requiring that accounts be kept in specified ways
and that payments be made only under certain circumstances.
Added to these limitations are the many legislative restrictions
on freedom of authority, such as limitations on the number of
promotions one person may be given in a single year, prohibi-
tions on the expenditure of funds for certain specified purposes, and a multitude of others.

Within an agency, similar restrictions on managers below the agency head are always found. Thus, such managers may not be permitted to speak freely to the press, or they must pay their employees salaries set by personnel offices, negotiate contracts written by lawyers not reporting to them, and so forth. For reasons of economy, consistency, or just the top man's personal interests, subordinate managers are rarely if ever given "authority commensurate with responsibility".

In private business, the same is true. Division vice–presidents may be held responsible for profit goals. But rarely are they given full authority for industrial relations, for legal services, for public and community relations.

O. Glenn Stahl has cogently stated this point as follows:

> It is futile to pontificate that every operator must have *authority commensurate with his responsibility* so that he can be held accountable. This is usually interpreted as freedom from restraints and limitations of various sorts; yet these very restraints and limitations are *part of the responsibility,* not something extraneous to it. We must come to the view that the director of a public program is responsible not just for program ends, but for achieving them *within* the controls, however wise or pointless they seem to be at the moment, that are established by legislative, judicial, or higher administrative authority.[26]

Thus it would appear that the "principle" of authority commensurate with responsibility must be compromised with other "principles", such as achieving economy, consistency, and uniformity of pay.

Many specific cases come to mind of jobs where responsibility is great and authority not-so-great. Staff units that have been given advisory functions only, for example, are responsible for doing a good job in their respective fields though they have no formal authority and must rely on such techniques as persuasion and knowledge. Coordinators (now frequently called "program managers", "product managers", or "project managers") are given responsibility for getting people to work together, but are usually not given formal authority to order them to do so and are almost never given full "line" authority over all the functions necessary to achieve success.[27] A person may be made responsible for completing an agency or company annual report of high quality by a specific date, but he often will not have the authority to *require* different parts of the enterprise to submit needed materials by that date.

There are other difficulties with the concept of commensurate authority and responsibility. One is that if an executive is responsible only to the extent of his authority, and his authority is over only one segment of the enterprise, then it follows that he need feel no sense of responsibility for the success of the rest of the enterprise (i.e., the enterprise as a whole)! I take it as fairly certain that most top executives would not want their lieutenants to feel this way. Similarly, if one accepts the frequent assertion that staff units have no formal authority (but only the "authority" of knowledge and persuasion), then it follows that staff units have no responsibility!

Another difficulty is that of determining quantitatively how much authority equates with how much responsibility. Suppose that a purchasing officer, for example, has authority to approve all purchases under $10,000. If the number of purchases he can approve doubles through greater workload, then presumably his responsibility (at least in financial terms) has doubled. But what about his authority? Is it the same (i.e., approval of purchases under $10,000) or is it doubled (i.e., approval of twice as many purchases)?

One astute observer of organizational life has summed up his reaction to the principle that authority should be commensurate with responsibility by referring to it as one of the most persistent myths of organization theory, and stating that "The idea seems to have persisted because it fits in with an accounting approach to organization".[28]

AUTHORITY AND DECENTRALIZATION

Mr. Fisher's third "simple and obvious" rule is that authority to act should be as close as possible to the level at which the work is performed. Since this principle relates to decentralization, which is covered in more detail in Chapter Three, I will treat of it only briefly here. In the first place, the words "as possible" mean different things to different people. How would this principle help us decide, for example, whether a board of directors (which is not very close to where the work is done) should approve all capital expenditures over $10,000, over $100,000, or over $500,000? Under Mr. Fisher's doctrine, it is likely that the decision in Korea would have been left to General MacArthur rather than to President Truman, who was far removed.

Again the problem is that while there are substantial benefits to having decisions made close to the work level under some circumstances, there are severe penalties to doing it under other circumstances. Decisions are often made at higher levels simply because they are important decisions (e.g., ones involving potentially great losses or gains) and must be made by those with the capacity to be more often right than wrong. When this is done, there are, of course, converse penalties. One such penalty might be that the people below would not be "developed" as well as they could be; another that decisions would take longer to be reached.

We have now seen that Mr. Fisher's three "simple and obvious" rules of organization are far from universally applicable. To elaborate on my point just a bit further, I would like to examine two of the most sacred and unquestioned "principles" of organization, to wit, that each person should report to only one boss, and that responsibilities should be clearly defined.

The One–Boss Rule

The "principle" that each person should report to only one boss is perhaps the most frequently and categorically verbalized of the so–called principles,[29] while at the same time being possibly the most often violated in practice.[30] One common example is the secretary who works for more than one person. Another example, at the other end of the spectrum, is the president of a company who reports to a board of directors, or perhaps the President of the United States, who reports to the public as a whole. To take an example somewhere between the secretary and the president, a ship commander in the Navy takes orders from the type commander on *how* to run his ship, but from the fleet commander on *where* to run it.[31] The National Aeronautics and Space Administration, still another example, has been consciously organized with multiple bosses and its administrator, James E. Webb, has pointed out that people uncomfortable under such a system would find it difficult to operate effectively in NASA.[32]

Let's take a typical example of multiple bosses, the Organization and Procedures Department of The Port of New York Authority, and follow it through in more detail. This department is made up of a director, a deputy director, a series of professional management analysts classified into grades (such as senior, intermediate and junior), and clerical help. The analysts form a pool and are assigned to specific projects as necessary. In simplified form, showing only five projects and five analysts, the organization chart of the department might appear as in Figure 9.

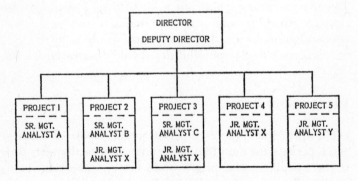

FIGURE 9. SCHEMATIC OF ORGANIZATION AND PROCEDURES DEPARTMENT

It is clear from this chart, that junior management analyst X has four bosses. On Project Four he reports to two of them: the director and the deputy director. On Project Three, he reports to senior management analyst C, and on Project Two he reports to senior management analyst B. Does this cause problems? Certainly. For example, he may sometimes find it difficult to divide his time in accordance with the wishes of all his bosses. He may find himself playing one boss off against another. But these disadvantages are by far outweighed by the advantages, principally: the flexibility of this type of organization in allowing analysts to be shifted around as needed; the ability to bring special skills to bear as needed; and the closer relationship between the junior people and the top departmental management on at least some of their activities.

As can be seen from the chart, even the senior management analysts have at least two bosses, the director and deputy director. Again there are advantages and disadvantages, but the net result for us is clearly to have a deputy to share the responsibilities of the director.[33]

In addition to this type of situation involving more than one boss, there are others. Every staff unit given a control function is, in one sense, the boss of the persons over whom this control is exercised. It is true that decisions by such staff units are usually subject to appeal; but, so usually are the decisions of your formally designated superior, and it simply isn't practicable to appeal most of the routine and numerous control decisions made by all the staff units.

Two other situations commonly involve more than one boss. One is when your immediate supervisor's own supervisor "by–passes" the intervening level to deal directly with you. In such cases, his orders must ordinarily be followed. The second case is that of the informal leader of the group who for certain purposes may become "the boss" of a group just as much as the formal supervisor is the boss for other purposes.

An unusual, but interesting, story of still another "boss" is told about a Federal Civil Service Commission personnel classification analyst who refused to change his decision on a particular job in a particular agency. The agency people threatened to go to his supervisor. "I don't work for him", the analyst replied. So the agency said they would carry their appeal to the Commission itself. "I don't work for them either", was the retort. "All right, then we'll go to the President", exclaimed the agency representative. "I'm sorry", came the answer, "but I don't work for him". "Who in the devil do you work for then?", he was asked. The clincher came back: "The Classification Act of 1923, as amended".

This story is not as far–fetched as it might seem. At a recent international conference on motivating the public servant, I delivered a paper which recommended, among other things, that periodic within–grade salary increases for civil servants be given in varied amounts based on performance, rather than in uniform amounts based merely on duration of service. Under any such plan, the supervisor would undoubtedly have to play a role in assessing performance. The reaction of a number of Europeans was that such a plan would cause the employee to curry favor with his supervisor by doing things as he wanted them done, rather than as the law required. A similar reaction can be found among teachers in this country whenever the subject of merit increases is raised.

The Clearly-Defined Responsibility Rule

The principle that responsibilities should be clearly defined has been questioned only in recent years. The argument for the principle is that ill–defined or vague responsibilities lead to jurisdictional conflict, difficulties in pinpointing accountability, confusion, and failure of anyone to "pick up the ball" in certain areas.

Rensis Likert, Director of the Institute of Social Research at the University of Michigan, however, has raised some thought–provoking questions concerning this concept.[34] He says, for example, that defining responsibilities rigidly and in detail tends to set up a wall between organization units, inhibit teamwork, foster loyalties to segments of the enterprise rather than to the whole, and force communications into a supervisor-subordinate pattern, as illustrated in Figure 10.

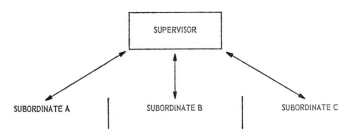

FIGURE 10. ORGANIZATION WITH CLEARLY DEFINED RESPONSIBILITIES

Under this man-to-man pattern of operation each subordinate benefits "by keeping as much information as possible to himself. Not only can he obtain decisions from his superior beneficial to himself, but he can use his knowledge secretly to connive with peers or subordinates against the others. In these ways, he is often able to increase his power and influence. He does this, however, at the expense of the total organization. . . . This [plan] operates to the disadvantage of the entire organization. Problems tend to be solved in terms of what is best for a department, not what is best for the company as a whole".[35]

Where responsibilities of each individual or unit are left more general, or even vague, it is alleged that the group tends to work more as a team. Each member of the group communicates with each other member, each tends to think in terms of the overall interest rather than that of his own organizational segment. There is less chance of anyone declining to act because "it isn't in my job description". This situation is illustrated in Figure 11.

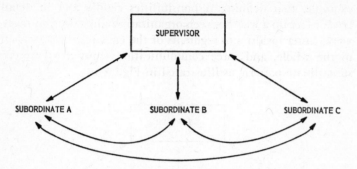

FIGURE 11. ORGANIZATION WITHOUT CLEARLY DEFINED RESPONSIBILITIES

The importance of not confining one's attention to his formally defined responsibilities has been well stated by John J. Corson as follows:

> The tradition that it is not right to invade the other fellow's bailiwick is a deterrent to innovation. Lucius D. Clay shocked an audience a few years ago when he asserted that the man on his staff who got ahead was the fellow who, seeing a need unmet or a problem unsolved, took it on himself to do something about it no matter whose province it technically fell in. He knew the implications of fearing to trangress organizational lines because of social pressure.[36]

Furthermore, it strikes me that too much emphasis on "responsibility and accountability" frequently leads to concentration of effort on fixing blame when a problem has arisen or a mistake has been made, rather than on working out a solution to the problem or developing methods of preventing similar mistakes in the future.

There appear to be powerful arguments on both sides of the question of clearly defining responsibilities. The trick is to know when to follow the classical principle, when to follow Likert, or how to compromise somewhere in between.

Do Principles of Organization Have Any Value?

Each of the traditional principles of organization could be analyzed in the same way with the same result. In each case we would find that under some conditions the principle is valid, while under other conditions it is not. Since I don't have time to cover each, I have tried in Appendix C, "Mutable Principles of Organization", to restate some of the most important of the classical principles in less doctrinaire form, and to list some of the considerations or factors governing the use of each.

Where does all this lead us with respect to the value of the traditional principles of organization? Are they of any practical use to the manager as guides to organizing? In their present form, I think they are of very little use. I am reminded of the so–called traits approach to effective leadership, which tries to identify good leaders by their traits or characteristics. This approach is now generally regarded as sterile and has virtually been abandoned.[37] Too many effective leaders have been found who lack some of the "requisite traits", or who exhibit varying combinations of traits depending on the situation. Similarly, too many effective organizations have been found that violate many of the traditional principles of organization, or which adopt different sets of principles in different circumstances.

It strikes me that organization theory in its present state is roughly comparable to the theory of raising children. In the latter case, there are certain gross rules which have some utility. For example, either physical beatings every day on the one hand, or giving into every whim of a child on the other, usually interferes with the child's becoming a mentally healthy adult. But apart from such extremes, there is a large area of behavior that can legitimately vary depending on the child, the parents, the environment, and the values of the person formulating the rules. Thus, it could well be that children who have disturbed relationships with their parents tend to grow up to

be more creative than children who have close, warm relationships with their parents. Some might argue, on the basis of such
a "fact", that parents should therefore strive for poor relationships with their children.

Similarly in organization. Making everyone in a large enterprise responsible for everything would tend to lead to chaos.
Adopting rigid rules governing responsibility for every detail
of work would tend to lead to stultification. But, again, there
is a large area of discretion where action depends on a multitude of variables and values. And who can say whether X
amount of efficiency obtained by organizing in one way is
better or worse than Y amount of democratic responsiveness
obtained by organizing in another way? Who's to say whether
a school system organized to achieve economy is absolutely better or worse than one organized to achieve racial balance?

There may be certain actions, in both the family and the enterprise, whose consequences can be predicted in terms of likeli-
hood. But people in an enterprise, like people in a family, are
individuals, not statistics. And decisions taken to accomplish
a given purpose must be made in relation to the particular
needs, values, and culture of the individuals comprising an enterprise or a family. Clearly defining the objectives and values
of a particular family or a particular enterprise is an essential
first step for arriving at workable decisions, including organizational decisions. But at present, such decisions generally involve
a large element of subjective judgment and common sense.
Surely many mistakes are made, but fewer, in my view, than
would be made by blind acceptance of current theory.

What clearly is needed before organization theory can reach
its full value is sufficient empirical research to demonstrate
under what conditions each principle of organization is valid.
Stated in terms of Herbert Simon's "mutually contradictory
pairs", we need to know under what conditions principle "A"
obtains and under what conditions its opposite obtains.[38] The
little research of this nature that has been done has generally

focussed on organization in the small face-to-face work group rather than on the agency or company as a whole.

One very hopeful example of the type of research that is needed is currently being undertaken jointly by the Research Committee on the Inter–University Case Program and the Institute of Governmental Studies, University of California.[39] This study involves preparation and analysis of some eleven case studies of specific governmental reorganizations. One of the purposes of the study is to test the following hypothesis (as well as three sub–hypotheses):

> Government reorganizations involving intended changes in individual behaviors are more effective, substantively, when the persons whose behaviors are expected to change participate in deciding what the change will be and how it will be made.[40]

The obstacles to success in this research are great. The variables other than participation that may affect the *success of reorganization* are numerous and complex. The variables that may affect the *success of participation* are also numerous and complex. Just trying to determine objectively that a reorganization is in fact "successful" or "unsuccessful" is a frightfully formidable problem. The very language of administration and organization is ambiguous and ill–defined. The hypothesis may be true, partially true, or false under different circumstances, such as level of government, size and level in the hierarchy of the unit being reorganized, type of work being performed, age and relative stability of the unit, real reasons behind any reorganization, and nature and personality of the key executives. The difficulty of getting the real story behind any reorganization including the personal and political factors as well as all the subtleties involved is well–nigh impossible.[41] And, of course, it's always possible that while participation may have achieved acceptance, it was acceptance of the wrong (or, at best, less than optimum) solution.[42] This is a frequent occurrence where maximum participation is sought, since solutions then tend to be compromises intended to "satisfy" all power centers—and a compromise is not always the optimum solution.

But the path is clear. The variables must be identified and in some manner weighed; the (almost) whole story must be obtained. Otherwise, managers concerned with organization will have to continue to operate in the dark, whether "by the seat of their pants", "by rule of thumb", or "by guess and by God". Undoubtedly some element of personal judgment—needed to take into account the intangibles, the subtleties, and the ambiguities in any complex organization problem—will always remain, even after more scientific propositions have been developed. But the extent to which this subjective element can be reduced is precisely the extent to which management theory may be able to help the practicing manager.

Until we have better data based on empirical research of this type, the principles are, as I have said, of little value as universal rules on how to organize. One of the troubles is that each new writer in the field proposes new and different "eternal principles". Perhaps the best that today's manager can do, when faced with an organization problem, is to use the so-called principles as a check list, or set of considerations to be kept in mind as a provisional frame of reference. Thus, in deciding in favor of one principle or its opposite, or more likely deciding on some compromise between them, he can at least make his decisions with a conscious knowledge of some of the gains and losses to be expected, and he may even be able to find ways of minimizing the losses. For example, if he follows the principle of clearly defining responsibilities in detail, he might try to find methods to counteract the tendency of this organizational decision to inhibit cooperation.

As we have seen, the classical principles of organization are in conflict with each other and each may be valid under certain circumstances, but not under others. In addition, these principles focus almost entirely on efficiency and economy which have turned out to be relatively minor considerations in most of our contemporary major organization decisions, as we shall see.[43] After each principle, one might well add the words, "other things being equal". The trouble is, "other things" (personalities, power, status, morale, traditions, etc.) are never equal.

THE PRAGMATIC APPROACH

This brings me to the approach which, in the present state of the art, seems to me to be the only realistic one available—that is, pragmatism, or doing what "works" in the particular situation, with due regard to both short and long range objectives.

I include long range objectives because pragmatism that focuses only on short range objectives, degenerates into expediency. I would like to emphasize that pragmatism does not mean (to me, at least) throwing out theory. It means, rather, knowing and using theory to the extent that it works, but not using it when it doesn't. Otherwise, pragmatism degenerates into nothing more than trial and error. (This may in itself have great advantages in creativity and innovation, but at enormous cost in time and money.) Someone once said—and I agree—that there is nothing as practical as a theory that works.

Of course, what works may or may not be desirable depending on the set of values one has. Thus, what "works" for one executive may be whatever gets better service or saves money; what "works" for another may be whatever doesn't present him with any unpleasant personnel problems even if it is costly or inefficient. The usual organization answer is a compromise that doesn't achieve the most of any one objective, but doesn't create an unbearable situation with respect to any other objective.

The best first-sergeant I came across during five years of army service used to say that army manuals were to be used when your brains ran out. This was not the reaction of the anti-intellectual who was against books, for this sergeant did understand and appreciate the values of manuals and did use them to good effect for training purposes. But he insisted that decisions be made to suit the circumstances and when something went wrong the fact that it had been done "by the book" was not an acceptable excuse. Men killed unnecessarily because the manual was followed when it should not have been are just as dead as those killed unnecessarily when the manual was not followed and should have been. Fortunately, many, if not most, American soldiers were pragmatists—as witness the derisive saying in the army that there are two ways of doing things, the army way and the right way. Managers, too, tend to be pragmatists in action if not in words. Like the proverbial farmer who claimed to be farming better than he knew how, most managers do a better job of organizing than they know how to do!

Organizational decisions are usually more or less rational responses to an interplay of ever–changing forces within the enterprise, in the environment, and between the enterprise and its environment. Effective organization involves continuous adaptation to a dynamic situation, and changes in the organization can be viewed as responses to actual or anticipated changes in the relationship among these forces. The study of organization, therefore, should concern itself with an understanding of those forces which are revelant and of their dynamic interplay.

Some of the most important of these forces are:

1. The enterprise's objectives and purposes, stated and implied.

2. The nature of the work to be done.

3. Technology, technological change, and the level of technological skills available to the enterprise.

4. The technological and formal interrelationships within the enterprise.

5. The psychology, values, and attitudes that prevail within the enterprise, particularly those of top management.

6. The interpersonal and sociological relationships within the enterprise.

7. Outside forces, such as changes in the economy, in competition, in technology, in laws, in labor relations, in the political situation and in broad sociological and cultural patterns.

Since all of these forces are in constant flux, it is well to reassess the organization pattern periodically. The very design of the organization structure is a significant force in the total situation, and changes in it can alter the total situation.

But there can be no ideal design or ideal arrangement that will fit all times, all situations, all objectives, and all values. The principles of both the "scientific management" and the "human relation" schools represent attempts to define such ideal arrangements. Both schools have suffered from a view of organization as an essentially static phenomenon or, if it is in motion, as moving in a straight line, and from their selection of one or another of the forces in the situation as being the only relevant one to be considered.

I suggest that the task of organization theory is not to lay down "principles", but to determine as precisely as possible what effects different arrangements of structure or process will have for a particular enterprise, staffed with real people, over a specified time period. This does not imply any evaluation of these effects in terms of universal ideals. Whether the effects are good or bad depends on the value system of those who are making the judgment. Organizational decisions require hard choices; and what favors certain groups or individuals usually penalizes others.

In the field of organization, the critical and compelling reasons for the decisions made are certainly subject to analysis, but they are usually peculiar to a particular enterprise or program and are usually not drawn from organization theory. I'd like to demonstrate this by reviewing briefly a recent major organization problem we faced in the Port Authority, and the principal factors affecting the organizational decisions made.

Several years ago, the states of New York and New Jersey enacted legislation authorizing the Port Authority to acquire, rehabilitate, and operate the Hudson and Manhattan (H & M) Railroad—a run-down, interstate commuter railroad that had been in bankruptcy for a number of years.

Some important background factors were relevant to the problem of how to organize for this new job.

To begin with, the H & M had been a going organization for over a half century, with more than 1,100 employees in a complex of parent and subsidiary corporations. Both its physical plant and its equipment were in extremely poor condition and needed wholesale rehabilitation or replacement. While the Port Authority had assumed responsibility for other long-established facilities, the H & M would be by far the largest, and its immediate rehabilitation needs the greatest.

Second, in contrast to the right-of-way or terminal operations that were characteristic of other Port Authority facilities, the H & M, serving over 100,000 passengers on an average weekday, was engaged in the task of actually carrying passengers from one terminal to another.

Third, H & M wages, working conditions, and work rules were spelled out in detail in union contracts, which placed great emphasis on seniority and rigidity of work assignments. Outside arbitrators and mediators were part of the collective bargaining process. And existing personnel relations between H & M management and labor reportedly were difficult.

Finally, the H & M's involvement with various federal control agencies, particularly the Interstate Commerce Commission, was substantial. Even personnel relations came under government auspices, collective bargaining being governed by the Railway Labor Act. Unlike the Port Authority, employment security benefits for most of the employees of the H & M were provided under the Federal Railroad Retirement Act and compensation for injuries under the Federal Employees Liability Act.

In addition to thse factors, there was a framework of Port Authority policies, as well as ICC and union requirements affecting organizational decisions. First, the executive director and the board of commissioners resolved that the acquisition of the badly run–down facility was to be followed by the development of a first class transit system. Second, all existing H & M personnel who wished to stay on were to be retained by the Port Authority. Third, labor relations with H & M employees were to be improved and brought up to the type normally enjoyed between the Port Authority and its employees. Fourth, existing union contracts were to be recognized by the Port Authority. This condition was a requirement set by the ICC and by the railway unions with which the H & M employees were affiliated. Fifth, the operation and rehabilitation of the railroad were to be integrated with existing functions of the Port Authority. Finally, the H & M's substantial involvement with federal regulatory agencies, it was determined, should be confined insofar as possible to H & M operations.

Three basic organizational questions arose, each of which I shall cover briefly in turn. The first was deciding upon the basic structure of the organization unit that would be given responsibility for H & M rehabilitation and operation. Three alternatives seemed possible: (1) to contract with an outside agency, (2) to assign the responsibility to a regular line department (new or existing) of the Port Authority, or (3) to establish a new subsidiary corporation within the Port Authority.

All three choices offered both advantages and disadvantages. The final decision was somewhat of a compromise. Basically it was to set up a subsidiary corporation (now known as the Port Authority Trans–Hudson Corporation), but to have it operate as much like a line department as possible within that framework, and to contract out several minor functions (e.g., selling and posting advertising displays).

The principal reasons for not using an outside agent, in addition to the fact that such an arrangement was not specifically authorized by the enabling legislation, were that a qualified contractor would be difficult (if not impossible) to find; contracting out would make it difficult to bring to bear Port Authority standards of efficiency and service; such action might open the Port Authority to public criticism on the grounds that it was trying to avoid a responsibility assigned to it; and a challenge exciting to the Port Authority staff would be missed.

The idea of direct assignment to a regular line department was discarded principally because assimilation of H & M staff with Port Authority staff would be extremely difficult owing to differences in personnel systems and union contracts, and because of the increased possibility of additional control by federal agencies over the Port Authority's non–railroad activities.

A subsidiary corporation, on the other hand, would make it possible to hold together the H & M staff and continue normal operations with minimum disruption, while the Port Authority staff became more familiar with the job of operating a commuter transit system; would help confine federal regulation to railroad operations; and would make the new operation a part of the Port Authority for purposes of providing a new "progressive" management climate, but separate enough to operate under its own personnel system, union contracts, and special legislation.

The second major organizational question was where to assign the new subsidiary—to an existing line department, to a new line department, or to the office of the executive director. Again, each possibility had its advantages and disadvantages. The decision was to assign it to a newly created line department—the Rail Transportation Department. In highly abbreviated form, the main reasons were that a new line department would offer a fresh approach to a new kind of activity; the existing line departments were busy on their own activities and had no railroad experience; a new complex operation was regarded as needing full attention at the department level without bogging down the executive director on details (if it reported directly to him); and there did already exist a highly qualified executive and a nucleus of staff in a Railroad Equipment Office (handling a program of providing commuter cars to the New York commuter railroads) which could be raised to departmental status.

The third major organizational problem was determining the relationships that should be established between existing H & M staff units (legal, medical, accounting, personnel, purchasing) and corresponding staff units in the Port Authority. Various alternatives again were available. The H & M staffs could be absorbed directly into the Port Authority staff departments, could remain a part of the new subsidiary reporting to its head, could remain a part of the new subsidiary but reporting to the department directors of their Port Authority counterpart staff departments, or some combination of these.

It was decided to integrate the legal staff directly with the Port Authority Law Department, and to leave the other staff units formally within the subsidiary corporation and physically located at its headquarters but otherwise integrated with their Port Authority staff department counterparts. The decision was based on several considerations: the fact that this arrangement provided a staff–line pattern familiar to the Port Authority made for easier adoption of Port Authority practices and procedures and for less jurisdictional conflict between the Port Authority staff departments and the new railroad line department. (The unavailability of key staff officials of the H & M was also a factor in the decision.)

Whatever the merits of the decisions that were made, the major considerations involved in them were situational, unique, and for the most part not directly related to traditional organizational theory or "principles".

Perspective

Psychologists have shown experimentally that one's state of mind directly affects one's perception of reality. Rapid shifts in perception based on changes in one's own situation are a common occurrence. I recall vividly from my college years before World War II how the Communists on campus emblazoned sidewalks and walls with the slogan "The Yanks are not coming". On the night of June 22, 1941, when Russia was invaded by Germany, these same students went around and added two words to the slogan, making it read "The Yanks are not coming too late".

Someone once said, "we see things not as they are, but as we are". Or as Rufus Miles put it, "Where one stands, depends on where he sits". This is as true for organization as for any other subject. Like the Texan's view of the map of the United States, or like the laboratory white mouse who claimed that he had the man-in-the-white-coat trained to give him a piece of cheese every time he ran through a certain maze, a person's view as to "proper" or "effective" organization depends upon his own vantage point. Rarely, if ever, is an organizational problem one of "good guys" *vs.* "bad guys". Rather, it is usually one between or among more or less decent people of different values and different self–interests, who see the problem from different perspectives.

I am reminded of Frank Pace (it could have been anyone else) when he was director of the U.S. Bureau of the Budget signing a report to the President recommending changes in the organization of the Panama Canal and Panama Railroad Company.[44] The report included a recommendation that responsibility for supervision of the Panama Canal and the Panama Railroad Company be transferred from the secretary of the army to the secretary of commerce. Shortly after he left the Bureau of the Budget to become secretary of the army, Pace wrote to the President objecting to some elements of the proposal he had approved as Budget Director, including the recommendation for transfer of supervising responsibility. This was neither hypocrisy nor fickleness, but rather a natural result of seeing the situation from a different angle.

One of the best organization analysts I ever knew frequently concluded from his organization studies that the basic problem as he perceived it was not one of organization but of communications. "If only people would talk to each other", he would lament, "there would be no problem". After he was promoted to a high level job in an operating department, he changed his tune. Now he would say that there just wasn't time to talk to all the people who were involved with his operations, and he would bemoan the fact that it was so difficult to imbue the various staff departments with the same sense of urgency and priority that he felt for his operations.

To take another example, the statement on "The Organization of the Port of New York Authority" (Appendix B) was sent in draft form to all Port Authority departments for review and comment. The typical reaction of the staff departments was that the statement portrayed staff departments as "second class citizens", and created in effect four separate Port Authorities by giving each of the (then) four line departments so much freedom that it could set its own standards, and adopt its own point of view without regard to the overall interests of the Port Authority, and build up its own staff services at the expense of the central staff departments. The typical reaction of the line departments, on the other hand, was that the draft statement made "second class citizens" of the line departments, gave them no freedom of action, subjected them to the control of too many bosses in the various staff departments, and gave them so little authority that they could not be held accountable for results.

A common, perhaps universal, difference of perspective exists between the top management of an organization, and that of its parts. This is a prime reason why decentralization, as we shall see in Chapter Three, can only be relative and never absolute. Take the example of a company which has "divisionalized" (that is, has organized on a product basis) and believes in maximum decentralization. Assume that the company goal for return on investment is 10 per cent. Assume further that Division A is currently making a return on investment of 8 per cent, that Division B is making a return on investment of 15 per cent, and that these are set as the goals for each Division. From the company point of view, a new product that would return 12 per cent should be added to the company line. Division A would no doubt agree. But Division B, if left to its own devices, would probably not initiate such a product because doing so would lower the average return on investment below the goal set for that division.

A similar example is where a division would prefer to buy materials or services from an outside vendor if it could get a better price, since its own record would look better, whereas buying from another division of the same company might hurt the record of the division doing the purchasing but make the overall company record better.

Thus, in considering whether a particular organization plan is successful, one must specify whether one means successful for the agency or company as a whole, or for some particular segment of it. And, as I have noted, one must ask, "successful" in relation to what values—productivity, profits, economy, satisfaction of employees, power, survival, and many others.

People so thoroughly believe that the organization should be the way they see it, and have usually rationalized their position so well that even a trained management analyst may have difficulty getting at the "truth" of the situation. Many times management analysts, after interviewing people in one department, have said to me that the answer seemed obvious, and that there was really no need for further interviews. After talking to interested parties in the other department or departments involved, however, an analyst may completely reverse himself and believe that the second view is the "correct" one. It is only after repeated discussions with *all* who have a legitimate interest in the problem, that an analyst can begin to recognize the complexities and the subtleties involved, to perceive that there is probably no one right answer for everyone and that no one (including himself) can ever see "total" reality, and to realize that the plan recommended will inevitably be the result of weighing many factors, hopefully resulting in more gains than losses.

In large part, the problem of perspective is the problem of

the specialist. As some one has said, "The specialist has a place in the scheme of things. He just doesn't know the scheme". It is natural for the specialist to regard his own sphere of action as far more important than it really is, and to interpret every phenomenon in terms of its effect on him, his operations, and his values.

So much for some of the problems inherent in the use of organization principles, the desirability of a pragmatic, or "situational", approach to organization, and the phenomenon of perspective. In Chapter Three I will focus on a number of more specific organization problems.

THREE

problems

Recently I saw a sign on an executive's desk which asked: "Are you here with the solution, or are you part of the problem?" In the field of organization, we have a wealth of problems (it not being unknown for some of them to be related to people). There are also a multitude of "solutions", but few, if any, "final answers".

In this chapter, I will deal with four perennial organizational problems:

1. Staff–line relationships
2. Centralization *vs.* decentralization
3. Delegation
4. Implementation of organizational change

Probably more words have been written, more panel discussions held, more heated bull sessions argued far into the night, and more doctrinaire positions advanced on these four problems than on any other aspects of organization. Yet let me hasten to assure any prospective Ph.D. students in search of a dissertation topic, that the definitive work has yet to be written on any of them. The field is wide open, and I invite any and all to try his hand at dispersing the fog and the nonsense that often surround each of these problems.

STAFF–LINE RELATIONSHIPS

The staff–line distinction has long been accepted as a fundamental tenet of organization theory. Yet, a group of top organization planners from industry and government in a recent two–day session on this topic couldn't identify or agree on any meaningful criteria to distinguish between staff and line.[45]

The main trouble, I believe, lies in a basic oversimplification of the problem. The orthodox view holds that "staff" thinks, plans, advises, persuades, has no formal authority, emphasizes the "how", and concentrates on long range factors, whereas "line" commands, acts, has formal authority, emphasizes the "what", and concentrates on short range factors.

I find that this generalization falls short of reality in many respects.

In the first place, it fails to recognize that there are different kinds of staff work, to which the descriptive adjectives listed above apply or do not apply in varying degrees. The most common types of staff work include:

1. Advice—e.g., recommendations of an organization planning staff to a department on a proposed reorganization.

2. Control—e.g., approval of a new form by a forms control unit or establishment of a job classification grade by a personnel unit.

3. Administrative services—e.g., preparing photostats or operating a library.

4. Specialized programs—e.g., management of debt, conduct of a community relations program, or handling of law suits.

5. Trouble shooting—e.g., a big part of the work of general staff assistants such as "assistants to".

The work of some staff units falls primarily in only one of these fields, but many staff units are engaged in several or all of them. A personnel department, for example, may "advise" on morale, "control" classification of jobs, and provide the "administrative service" of running a cafeteria.

Moreover, many units may combine line as well as staff elements. An interesting example can be found in the police function of The Port of New York Authority.

The Port Authority has its own police force, which has functions and authority similar to those of any municipal police force. Prior to a major reorganization of the Port Authority in 1952, there was a single unified police force in the Operations Department. The reorganization set up four separate line departments, apportioning some of the total of twenty–two facilities (i.e., airports, tunnels and bridges, marine terminals and land terminals) to each, and assigning responsibility for net revenues and public service to the line department directors and facility managers.

This reorganization presented a dilemma with respect to the police force. If it remained unified, then net revenue and service responsibilities of the line would be diluted. If it were split up and apportioned to the line departments or facilities, there would be four (or possibly even twenty–two!) separate police departments and a consequent loss in uniformity, morale, economy, promotion opportunities, and flexibility in a pooled operation of some 1,100 officers.

After careful study, the initial solution was a compromise. The facility manager was given full responsibility for supervision. He assigned jobs, rated performance, and directed results. He decided "how many" police he needed. He was responsible for the "what", "when", and "how many". A police superintendent, in charge of a central staff police division, was made responsible for the development of standards, training, and advising the facility manager on police requirements. He emphasized the "how" and the "who".

While the line departments were generally satisfied with this arrangement, the police were not. They did not fully understand the split, and they resisted having promotions and disciplinary actions handled by "civilians". After much soul searching, it was decided to assign responsibility for disciplinary proceedings and personnel ratings to the police commanding officer at each facility, but to stipulate that on these matters he was to report to the central superintendent of police at headquarters.

This compromise, plus strenuous efforts to educate all concerned as to how the system works, resulted in an effective and viable police operation.

I have gone into some detail on this example in order to illustrate the difficulty of deciding whether to designate the Port Authority police force as "staff", as "line", or as both, inasmuch as we decided to have a central "staff" police division while at the same time most of the police officers work in line capacities for line departments.

A second difficulty with the orthodox distinction is the failure to recognize that a staff unit has one relationship to the other segments (i.e., other staff and line units) of the enterprise, and another relationship to the chief executive. Take, for example, a staff unit, such as an organization and methods office, whose function may be in large part that of rendering advice to other departments. In this respect, the unit may fit the orthodox view. But the same unit reports to a boss (say, the chief executive), and likely assists him in planning and evaluating organization and methods for the enterprise as a whole. In this respect, the staff unit's relationship to the chief executive is the same as that of the line unit. The staff man may recommend that the chief executive approve an overall reorganization, just as the line man may recommend that the chief executive approve the plans for a new hanger at an airport. Both the staff and line executive are accountable to the chief executive for the success or lack of success of their recommendations. And both use similar methods of persuasion to get their superior to approve their proposals.

A third misconception arises from the very use of the words "staff–line relationships". For the problem is in reality "staff–clientele relationships". Thus, a personnel department has exactly the same relationship (i.e., exercises the same advisory, control, and service functions) to other staff departments such as the finance department or the organization and methods department, as it does to line or operating departments. And these other staff departments give the personnel department just as hard a time as the line departments do.

A fourth element of the oversimplified view of the staff–line problem is the failure to recognize that the problem is frequently really one of "level". What I mean here is that when there is conflict between a central staff unit and a line (or other staff) department, what the latter department may really be saying is that it would like this central staff function decentralized. The function might still be set up as a *staff* unit within the other department. Thus, for example, if the personnel function were decentralized to operating departments, these departments would be likely to set up personnel units (or individuals, depending on the size of the operation) which would be staff in relation to the various other sub–divisions of the department. In this light, the problem can be seen to be one of centralization *vs.* decentralization, rather than staff *vs.* line.[46]

And lastly, there has been a failure to recognize that the staff–line problem depends in part on the breadth of one's point of view. Thus, the U.S. Bureau of the Budget, looked at in relation to the federal government as a whole, is a staff unit. But within the bureau, it has its own line divisions and staff units. And looked at internally, the director of the Bureau of the Budget (or any other staff unit) has the same responsibilities as the head of any line department or bureau. They both must plan work, direct and motivate their subordinates, evaluate the work being done, organize their unit, coordinate the work of the segments of the enterprise.

Many other attempts have been made to provide a simple distinction between line and staff, besides the orthodox position which I have already described.

One commonly expressed view is that "line" units are those which carry out the basic functions of the enterprise (i.e., what it is set up to do), while "staff" units are created to provide assistance to them. This distinction is not very helpful in many cases. An agency sending technical assistance to underdeveloped countries, for example, could be organized with "country desks" as the line units, and fields of assistance (e.g., agriculture, health, education) as staff units, or vice versa. Both specialties are necessary, and neither can be solely identified with what the agency is set up to do.

Even in business which is set up to make a profit, the distinction is not clear–cut. Investments and purchasing, commonly regarded as staff functions, are certainly closely related to profits. Even industrial relations, universally regarded as staff, can make or break a company by the wages it arrives at, by its policies on treatment of employees, or by actions which may cause or prevent a serious strike.

Another distinction which has been proposed is based on responsibility, or accountability, which supposedly lies with the line. However, it seems to me that in large organizations, at least, complex decisions are nearly always the result of an interchange of views among many key people, with the decision, and the accountability, in reality shared. Such decisions generally depend on legal, financial, public relations and operating considerations—and bad advice on any of these grounds could bring about sour results. Edward C. Schleh, among others, has pointed out graphically how important decisions involve dual responsibility of both line and staff.[47]

Moreover, any attempt to pinpoint responsibility on one person or unit for certain decisions may tend to foster irresponsibility on the part of other persons or units who may then feel removed from involvement.[48]

Because of the many types of staff, as outlined above, responsibility for particular actions may, in fact, lie principally with a staff unit, principally with a line unit, or be shared by both.[49]

Another distinction which has been made is based on who appeals—i.e., when line and staff disagree, it is incumbent upon staff to appeal. However, this can work either way. When staff has advisory functions, it is true that the burden of appeal lies with it. But when staff has control functions, the burden of appeal usually lies with the line (or other staff) department. Moreover, it seems to me that the distinction is academic, for regardless of who initiates the appeal, both parties usually go to their common superior (whether together or separately) to get the conflict resolved.

One final distinction, commonly made, relates to the type of person found doing "line" or "staff" work. Early writers, basing their findings on manufacturing, characterized line people as practical, less highly educated, less articulate, located in the plant, and with loyalties to the company. Staff people on the other hand, were said to be theoretical, more highly educated, articulate, professional, white collar (office), and with loyalties to their profession. We now recognize that the reverse can be true. Thus in a school, the line people are the teachers—who tend to be highly educated, professional, white collar, with loyalties to their profession; the staff people, who are largely in administrative and maintenance jobs, are less well educated, blue or white collar, with loyalties to the school or city rather than to a profession. Hospitals tend to be like schools in this respect.

Or to take a technical assistance agency again, any such distinction as to the kind of people found on the geographic desks or in the subject matter fields would be difficult to perceive, even if one could decide which was line and which was staff.

The writer who has made the most sense to me in this field of staff–line relationships is O. Glenn Stahl. He has stated:

> In conclusion, then, would it not make sense to divest ourselves of the abracadabra that divides "line" and "staff" into incongruous kinds of activity and to recognize that *all* such activities are simply specialized subdivisions of an organization's work?
>
> *I find it convenient to think of the work of an enterprise as a network, a grid, or a check-board in which vertical program subdivisions are interlaced with horizontal sustaining activities. The chief executive sits in a position at a top corner from which he holds both the vertical lines and the horizontal lines. They are*

all lines; for controls are exercised in both directions at once. Where they intersect there is potentiality for conflict or at least the necessity for reconciliation, but such a conception breeds the settlement of issues where they are first detected. This constitutes half the dynamics of running an organization.

No purpose is served in fighting this phenomenon in the name of confining staff and line to their respective hypothetical roles. Let's relax and enjoy it! It at least saves us from guilt complexes, makes everyone's behavior more open and above board, lubricates communication channels, and facilitates decision–making at a given point in the hierarchy on the common–sense basis of a combination of the requisite information and capacity, without preoccupying us with who has the right to do what to whom.[50]

In my judgment, the key to effective staff–line relationships lies in the following areas.

First, and perhaps most important, avoid talmudic discussions of "correct" staff–line theory and philosophy. Decide instead how your particular enterprise wants to work, what you want to be designated as staff and what as line, what their functions shall be, and how they shall interrelate. Then educate all concerned on your decision. It would be well to follow the advice of Humpty Dumpty who said: "When I use a word, it means just what I choose it to mean—neither more nor less."[51] See Appendix B, especially Paragraph V, for the criteria adopted by one agency to govern staff–line relationships.

Second, recognize that conflict between line and staff is desirable if it brings to bear on the solution of problems different perspectives and points of view, rather than merely jurisdictional jealousies. The result is to make it possible to arrive at decisions based on more complete information, and to bring problems up to the proper level for decision where staff and line cannot agree.

Third, establish an overall management climate which emphasizes results, teamwork, and loyalty to the enterprise as a whole rather than just to segments of it.

And fourth, where feasible, avoid assigning incompatible roles to the same staff units. For example, to the extent possible, separate the advisory role from the inspection and audit role, and from the performance of routine auxiliary services.

A fifth suggestion, strongly supported by some, is to rotate key executives between staff and line positions. The rationale is that such rotation will help the executives to understand both roles and thus enable them to work together more effectively. While I do not oppose this approach, for it undoubtedly broadens the executive, I am somewhat skeptical as to results insofar as reducing staff–line conflict is concerned.

For one thing, the success of such a plan depends again on what staff functions we are talking about. Rotation into highly technical positions such as legal and medical, for example, is generally not feasible. For another, I personally have not noticed any exceptional results from this approach. Staff units usually are just as demanding and as "tough" on other staff units as are line units—which should not be the case if having served in staff work helped one to get along with staff units. I am reminded of the cliché in the army that having served as an enlisted man would make one a better officer (again, because theoretically such an officer would understand the enlisted man's point of view). In fact, I could see no such cause–effect relationship. Many officers who had been enlisted men seemed to take the view that "they [the officers] took advantage of me when I was an enlisted man, now it's my turn to do the same".

Moreover, as I have stated, the purpose of good staff–line relationships is not to reduce conflict but to raise it to a higher and more meaningful level.

CENTRALIZATION vs. DECENTRALIZATION

In recent years, "decentralization" seems to have become practically a principle of organization rather than a description of how a particular organization is functioning. Thus, many writers state *as a principle* that decisions should be made at the lowest practicable level.[52] This view has been supported by the devotees of the human relations school of thought who seem to be interested more in the development of people and in so–called participative management than in achieving the (other) objectives of the enterprise.

While I am not aware of any detailed study of the extent of decentralization in government or industry as a whole, there is considerable evidence that there has been a long–time trend toward decentralization. This does not mean, however, that the net balance is in that direction. As late as 1955, Ernest Dale, probably the most knowledgeable person in the country on this subject, said: "Centralization is still quite widespread. Probably 'one man control' is found in more companies and affects more employees than 'control by the few' or 'control by the many' ".[53]

Interestingly, in recent years a number of observers have reported finding a counter–trend back toward centralization, sometimes called recentralization.

What I would like to do in this section is try to clear up some confusion as to the meaning of the terms "centralization" and "decentralization"; account for some of the reasons why certain enterprises have decided to recentralize; review some of the gains and losses from decentralizing; and identify some of the long–term factors affecting centralization and decentralization and where they are apt to lead.

In attempting to define "centralization" and "decentralization", a number of preliminary problems have to be recognized and disposed of. In the first place, many writers have confused decentralization with reorganizations involving a change from the process or functional type of organization to the product or purpose type.[54] They are not the same. It is true that such a re-organization usually makes it *easier* to decentralize (since the top man is relieved of some of his coordinating problems and can more easily fix responsibility and accountability on the level immediately below him); however, even under the purpose or product type organization, the top man may still retain all essential decision–making functions. He may, for example, continue to review all personnel promotions, purchases or contracts above any given dollar value.

Moreover, even if the chief executive did decentralize a portion of his decision–making responsibilities to the level below under the new organization, his subordinates may well continue to run their divisions on a highly centralized basis, thus accomplishing a degree of decentralization, but leaving the total enterprise more centralized than decentralized.

An interesting dilemma presents itself here. Suppose the agency head or company president strongly believes in decentralization as a way of life. Theoretically, then, he should decentralize to his immediate subordinates the right to organize their divisions as they see fit. But if they, on the other hand, believe in centralization, and organize their divisions on a centralized basis, they are defeating the will of their superior. If he insists that his subordinates decentralize their own divisions, he has "centralized" by taking away their right to make their own decisions on this matter!

One further implication of the change from process to product or purpose organization is that inevitably the change can never be a total one. For purposes of economy, consistency, and control, and because of the need to make certain decisions on the basis of the interests of the enterprise as a whole, a number of staff units will always be retained on a centralized basis. Looked at in this way, the problem of decentralization becomes in large part the problem of defining the role of the central staff units.[55]

A second problem in attempting to reach an adequate definition of centralization and decentralization involves the necessity to distinguish between the "level" at which a particular decision is made and the number of people authorized to make the decision. To illustrate, an agency head might delegate the authority to approve promotions of all personnel below a certain salary either to the personnel director, or to *all* subordinates reporting directly to the agency head. In both cases, he has delegated to the level below himself. However, in one case such decisions are still concentrated in the hands of one man, while in the other case it is parceled out to many.

A third problem is to distinguish between the level of decision–making and geographic decentralization. The term "geographic decentralization" has frequently been used to mean the geographic dispersal of facilities and people unrelated to any change in their decision–making authority. Moreover, when decision–making is decentralized to geographically separated units, there is sometimes a tendency to establish more controls than when decentralizing within a particular headquarters because of the anxiety raised by physical separation.

A fourth, and very common, problem is to talk about centralization and decentralization as though they were absolute concepts. In any sizeable enterprise, this is an unrealistic view. The terms are "relative" rather than "absolute" in at least four ways: (1) They are always a matter of degree—all decisions of all kinds can never in actuality be made only at the very top or at the very bottom of any enterprise consisting of more than one, or a few, persons; (2) the amount of centralization or decentralization must be assessed at each level—as has been noted, the top man may decentralize broadly to his subordinates, some of whom may and some of whom may not decentralize broadly to their subordinates, and so on down the hierarchy; (3) the extent of centralization or decentralization varies by function, it being possible and even likely that some functions (say personnel and purchasing) may be relatively centralized while others (say engineering and graphics) may at the same time be relatively decentralized; and (4) the extent of centralization or decentralization varies with time, the actual situation being constantly in flux.

A fifth problem is that of perspective: from whose point of view does one determine whether a particular change is in the direction of centralization or decentralization? Thus, the addition of a new level of group vice presidents between the existing president and vice presidents is frequently spoken of as a move toward decentralization. This is because, from the president's point of view, some decisions formerly made by him are now made below his level. However, to the extent that the new

group vice presidents are making decisions formerly made by
the vice presidents, this would be a pretty clear-cut case of centralization from the point of view of the vice presidents.

A final problem related to definition is the need to draw a
sharp distinction between "apparent" and "real" decentralization (or centralization). For example, the formal rule may be
that the head of an agency must approve all personnel promotions involving salaries over $5,000. If, in fact, he signs them
automatically without raising questions on any except those
at $12,000 or over, then the reality is that he has delegated de-
cision-making for all such promotions below $12,000. There
are many nuances involved in this distinction. Principally, these
involve the extent of policies and standards (written or un-
written, perceived by the boss or by the subordinates or both)
governing decisions, the known or perceived likes and dislikes
of superiors, the consequences (i.e., actions of superiors) when
mistakes are made, and the existence of alternative decisions
available to the decision-maker.

Taking into account all of these problems, I arrive at a definition that "centralization and decentralization are relative
terms based on the level at which decisions are actually made
and the number of decision-makers". This definition is closely
related to the concept of delegation which I will take up below.

As I have noted, some enterprises that had moved substantially toward decentralization later reversed their direction by
"recentralizing". (Some alleged recentralizations, however,
were in reality merely the adding of appropriate policies and
controls to make the decentralization more effective.)

There have been a number of reasons for such reversals. An
important reason in industry has been economic recession. A
number of companies which decentralized in the years preceding a recession found that the increased costs were not compensated for by increasing revenues. In other cases, poor results
may have been attributed to the decentralization although they
actually came about because of the recession. And in still other
situations, executives "running scared" during a recession may

have decided to recentralize just because they felt the need to take some major action in a period of bad times.

Another reason for recentralizing has been that the original decision to decentralize may have simply been the wrong decision for that enterprise. Perhaps it had been adopted merely because others were doing it, and not to meet any real, identifiable need.

A third reason is that the decentralization didn't work effectively, not because the idea was not good, but because it was mismanaged.[56] Thus, there may have been inadequate policies, controls and/or standards established (there is an old adage that you must centralize before you can decentralize); or conversely there may have been too rigid policies, controls and/or standards established; or the policies, controls and/or standards may not have been adequately defined or generally understood; or the degree of decentralization might have been too great or too little; or the subordinates involved might not have been ready to assume their new responsibilities.

A fourth reason for recentralization is that management may have expected too much too soon. Many of the expected benefits of decentralization, such as the development of people, are often a long time in coming.

In deciding upon the degree of decentralization that is desirable, the ultimate test for business would seem to be that in the long run increased profits must outweigh increased costs. Similarly, in government, the basic test would seem to be that improved service (or possibly improved democratic controls) must outweigh the increased costs.

In general, what one hopes to gain by moving in the direction of decentralization are such benefits as the following:

1. Faster decisions (because of fewer reviews and shorter lines of communications).

2. Better decisions (because the decision–maker is closer to the problem and has more of the facts in mind). But note that this can work the other way if the person at the lower level is less competent or doesn't see the relationship of his operation

to other related operations and this relationship is an important
factor affecting the decision.[57]

3. Development of people.

4. More original ideas.

5. Better morale.

6. Greater involvement, enthusiasm, drive and motivation.[58]

7. Easier acceptance of change.

8. More time for top executives to devote to major policy
and long range problems.

9. More clearly fixed responsibility (because less people in
the hierarchy are involved in the decision).

As in most of life, however, when you gain one thing, you
pay for it in some other way. The most likely penalties of decentralization are:

1. Increased costs (because decentralization usually means
the addition of staff and equipment). This may be partially offset by less need for vertical reviews.

2. Lower quality of decisions, at least in the short run. There
is more danger of mistakes if subordinates are less competent
or have a more narrow perspective, and decisions may be
made in the interest of the sub–group rather than the overall
enterprise.

3. Inconsistent policies or application of policies.

4. Less effective top executives (if they are unable to adjust
to operating by control and coordination rather than by issuing direct orders and by personal involvement in operations).

Probably the most basic issue in deciding whether to move
substantially in the direction of decentralization is that of more
effective performance *vs.* increased costs. While the initial
change to a relatively decentralized system is undoubtedly
costly, such costs will often be compensated for after a period
of years. In any event, decentralization is never absolute, but
rather a compromise. Thus, when decentralization is attempted
in conjunction with a reorganization from a process or function pattern to a product or purpose pattern, some staff services
and controls are inevitably kept on a centralized basis.[59] If the

central controls are too tight, the overall result is unlikely to be any great degree of decentralization. If the central controls are too loose, top management will have no assurance as to final results, and may well react by deciding to recentralize.

What is the future likely to see—more or less decentralization, more or less centralization? There are many forces that will affect the answer, one way or the other. Some of these, such as technological change, automation, size and composition of the work force, I have examined in more detail below.[60]

By and large, the forces that would seem to push toward further decentralization appear to me to include increased size of individual enterprises, continued diversification, the continued trend in business from ownership to managerial control, the increased proportion of more highly educated professional and white collar workers, increased knowledge about motivation theory, changes in the expectations of the work force (likely to be in the direction of democratic ideals), acceptance by more business managers of their social and civic responsibilities, the development of more effective methods for control and evaluation of results, and a prosperous economy.

Forces that will probably push toward centralization include the increased complexity and importance of managerial decisions (and their impact on society), the scarcity of executive talent in relation to need, and economic reversals such as a recession.

Forces that may result in either centralization or decentralization (depending on the circumstances) or the impact of which is not clear, include technological change (especially automation and electronic data processing), increased world competition (whether business or government), changes in the nature of the cold war, and changing patterns of labor-management relations.

The net result of all of these factors leads me to believe that the general trend will continue to be in the direction of decentralization.[61] But this is only in the very general and overall sense. Undoubtedly there will be a mixture of conflicting trends in different agencies or companies, by functions within an agency or company, and over a period of time.

The only plea I would make is that the degree of centralization or decentralization for a particular enterprise or function be determined pragmatically in terms of such factors as public convenience, economy, quality of service, availability of skilled personnel, need for control, and general effectiveness. Remember, however, that the pragmatic approach must consider the long-range survival of the enterprise as well as immediate results.

DELEGATION

The problem of delegation may be considered a special aspect of the problem of centralization *vs.* decentralization. Whereas the latter problem deals essentially with the locus of decision-making in the enterprise as a whole, delegation, in the sense that I am using it here, has to do with the relationship between an individual superior and his immediate subordinates. This relationship constitutes an important problem in organizing, since it deals with the division of work between vertical levels.

Considerable confusion has arisen in discussions of this problem because of lack of clarity as to just what is being delegated.

Is responsibility (i.e., duty) delegated? Yes, in the sense that by assigning a job to a subordinate, the latter is made responsible for it. But this does not in any way imply that the delegator divests himself of responsibility for the job being done. He retains that responsibility, but his role changes. Instead of doing the job himself, he becomes a trainer, a motivator and an evaluator. And he retains responsibility for delegating properly to a qualified subordinate.

Is authority (i.e., power) delegated? Yes, with the limitation that one ordinarily cannot delegate authority which he does not himself have. And since the delegator retains the right of

retracting his delegation, he does not completely divest himself
of authority.

Is accountability (i.e., being answerable for results) delegated? Yes, a new accountability is established in the sense that
the delegatee is now accountable to the delegator for results.
But, again, the delegator retains accountability to his own superior for results. In practice, accountability is shared. The
delegator is accountable for overall performance of his unit.
Individual mistakes may be blamed principally on the delegatee. Too many mistakes, however, will undoubtedly be
blamed on the delegator.

Perhaps it is most convenient to think of delegation as involving assignment of a portion of one's work. This does not
necessarily imply delegation of decision–making, since it might
involve merely fact–finding with no decision responsibility.
Ordinarily, there are certain tasks not considered delegable,
such as a supervisor's leadership, coordinating and evaluating
functions, although he may well have staff assistants helping
him with these tasks.

A major conceptual problem that has plagued many discussions of delegation is the assumption that delegation is a "do or
don't", a "go or no go" proposition. On the contrary, there are
many degrees of delegation. It might almost be envisaged as a
continuum with a whole range of relationships available depending on such factors as the personality of the superior, the
personality of the subordinate, the nature of their relationships,
the type of work or problem at issue, the time available, and
the amount of top management interest.

Typical degrees of delegation that might be used by a supervisor are:[62]

1. Take action—no further contact with me is needed.

2. Take action—let me know what you did.

3. Look into this problem—let me know what you intend to
do; do it unless I say not to.

4. Look into this problem—let me know what you intend to
do; delay action until I give approval.

5. Look into this problem—let me know alternative actions available with pros and cons and recommend one for my approval.

6. Look into this problem—give me all the facts; I will decide what to do.

Probably the most basic problem related to delegation arises from the fact that the authorities on the subject are practically unanimous in their belief that there ought to be "more" of it, whereas managers seem to be nearly as universally reluctant to delegate substantially. Management consultants frequently find in their surveys that supervisors at all levels report the same thing, saying "my boss doesn't delegate enough to me" but also saying "I can't delegate as much as I'd like to since my subordinates aren't competent". In a sense we have a "chicken and egg" proposition, with many practitioners saying they don't delegate because their subordinates aren't competent, while the theorists say that the subordinates aren't competent because there has not been enough delegation.

Since management theory tends to applaud substantial delegation, why has there been relatively little of it in practice? There seem to be two principal circumstances when there is relatively little delegation: when the superior is, or thinks he is, more competent than his subordinates, and when the superior is, or thinks he is, less competent than his subordinates.[63]

The superior who is, or who thinks he is, more competent than his subordinates tends to avoid delegation because of the inevitable pressure for "right" decisions. He knows, especially if he worked his own way up, that there is often much truth in the saying, "If you want something done well, do it yourself".

Nevertheless, no matter how competent he may be, it is the rare supervisor who can do all the work of his unit. Therefore, he must decide what and how much to delegate. In making this decision, some tests he might apply are:

1. How important is the decision? Are the stakes so high

that a mistake cannot be tolerated? If so, the matter cannot be delegated to any great degree.[64]

2. Even though the superior is more competent than a subordinate, is the superior close enough to the problem (i.e., does he have sufficient information about it) so that in fact his decision would be more apt to be right?

3. Does failure to delegate mean that the superior is not giving adequate attention to other more important parts of his job (i.e., is he working below his appropriate level)?

4. Does failure to delegate mean that the supervisor is not developing his subordinates? Are they developable? If not, can they be transferred or otherwise replaced?

5. What does top management really expect of the supervisor? Are they measuring him principally by current results, so that his decisions must be right? If they say they expect him to develop people, do they really mean it, or do his "antennae" tell him that their verbalizations are empty words, that they can't measure him on this score anyhow, or that the ultimate measure is so far in the future as to be of no real concern?

The supervisor who is, or who thinks he is, less competent than his subordinates, has other reasons for not delegating. In such cases, the supervisor is apt to be so insecure and anxiety-ridden that it is difficult for him to let subordinates show their stuff since they might "prove" that they are better than he is. He may try to prove to himself that he is better than his subordinates by reviewing their work in detail, often making petty changes, such as substituting a word or a punctuation mark here or there. He is generally unwilling or unable to take chances. And he may lack confidence in his own ability to direct others (i.e., plan work, formulate objectives, communicate with the subordinate) and finds it more "comfortable" to do the job himself.

There are many other circumstances that tend to inhibit delegation. These include the following:

1. Where the supervisor's own supervisor expects him to

know everything in detail, it will be hard for him to delegate.

2. The absence of adequate controls to give warning of impending difficulties will make delegation less feasible.

3. Some persons put in a supervisory role are more comfortable working with the substance of a problem than managing the work of others. This seems to be relatively more frequent among professionals such as engineers, lawyers and doctors.

4. When a unit grows rapidly in size, some supervisors find it easier to handle the problem by continuing their accustomed pattern of operation, only working harder and longer. They may not know how to work any other way, they may fear changing their familiar habits (just as so many people who have never used a dictating machine resist its adoption), or there might be just plain lag in the time it takes to adjust to the new situation.

5. The subordinates themselves may resist accepting more responsibility—either because of their own insecurities, because they are already overworked, or because they are not motivated to do more.

6. Where the overall climate of the enterprise is one of insecurity and uncertainty, and involves extreme penalties for making a mistake, delegation will tend to be limited.

7. Even where a particular supervisor may want to delegate, he may find that delegating a task to a junior requires that junior to deal with higher level people in other units who do not delegate. Such higher level persons are often "insulted" when a junior contacts them, and let the original delegator know it. (Thus, effective delegation depends not only on the delegator and delegatee, but also on the attitudes of others in the enterprise.)

There are some general guidelines that experience has shown are helpful for successful delegation. Some apply to the delgator, some to the delegatee, and some are the responsibility of the enterprise as a whole (and therefore of top management). These guidelines include the following:

1. To the extent possible, the delegator should delegate by results expected, not methods to be used. That is, the delegatee should be free to do the job his own way—so long as his actions do not violate some overall policy or cause other problems of consequence. This approach will work most effectively where performance standards have been set in order to provide a way of measuring results. A good example is the salesman's quota.

2. The delegator should give the delegatee all relevant information on the task delegated. He should establish a climate of free and open communication between himself and the delegatee, but make it clear that he expects "completed staff work".

3. Delegations should be made to qualified people. This implies, first, that capable people be recruited, trained, and motivated throughout the enterprise. Then, for the specific delegation, the delegator should make sure that the delegatee has the resources (skills, people, information, material) to do the job. Thus, the delegator must understand the abilities and limitations of each of his subordinates. But over a period of time he should have been giving them practice in accepting delegations (i.e., responsibility), and should understand that the question is not primarily whether the subordinate can do the job better than he can, but rather whether he can do it adequately, whether it is desirable for the development of the subordinate, and whether he (the superior) could or should be spending his time on more important matters.

4. The policies of the enterprise should be clearly spelled out. For example, if the promotion of personnel is to be delegated, policies regarding the emphasis to be given merit *vs.* seniority should be clear.

5. Controls should be established to alert the delegator at an early stage if things are getting out of control.

6. The overall climate set by the enterprise should be such that each supervisor knows that he is expected not only to be a "leader" (i.e., planner, organizer, decision maker, evaluator,

etc.), but also a developer of people and a member of a team whose job it is to maximize the resources of others.

Delegation is frequently, and accurately, spoken of as the "art of delegation". It is personal and individual. It depends on the informal relationships, largely the sense of trust and confidence, built between a superior and each of his subordinates. Ultimately, the degree to which a supervisor delegates is a matter of the net result of many factors. It will tend to be greater if the subordinate is competent and his development is a high value; it will tend to be less if the problem is crucial or complex and if time is of the essence.

Before leaving the subject of delegation, I want to say a few words about "by–passing", the process whereby a supervisor skips one or more intervening levels of supervision to deal directly with a person on a lower echelon.

It should be immediately apparent that by–passing is fraught with dangers. It can add to the insecurity of the intermediate person and perhaps undermine his effectiveness in the future; it can result in actions taken without information which perhaps only the person by–passed has; it can put the subordinate in a position of being told to do something in conflict with previous orders given by his immediate superior.

Nevertheless, some kinds of by–passing are undoubtedly justifiable. One, for example, is in case of emergency where there is danger to life or property and insufficient time to locate the intermediate supervisor. Another is where routine information (as distinguished from orders) is to be obtained or given.

The real reasons for by–passing, however, are frequently either lack of confidence in the "man in the middle" or a desire to save time and cut bureaucratic red tape. In the first case, a better answer is either to "buck–up" the intermediate supervisor (through counselling, training, disciplinary actions, etc.) or replace him if necessary. In the second case, the advantages of speed must be weighed against the disadvantages that I have already mentioned. The conclusion may depend in large part on the nature of the problem at hand and the relative security of the persons involved.

Other "justifications" for by–passing are when a high level manager wants to get firsthand exposure to individuals down the line, a "feel" of problems faced on the firing line, or technical explanations from highly specialized personnel on subjects which the intermediate supervisor isn't expected to have mastered. These needs, however, can usually be served by having the intermediate supervisor present at the same time.

Effectuating Organizational Changes

Herbert Kaufman, in his perceptive and highly useful case study of the New York City Health Centers,[65] begins as follows:

> In the year 1915, the Commissioner of Health of New York City decided to make a change in the way the work of his Department was carried on. Theretofore all its work had been handled by its specialized bureaus; thereafter the bureaus would be retained, work in the field would be carried out through district health offices, each under the supervision of a district health officer with general responsibility for health operations in his district.
>
> The decision was made and announced; but the decision was, in an important sense, still being made 44 years later, in 1959, and new announcements concerning the underlying decision were still being issued. At first glance, this may seem astonishing; but any decision that involves fundamental changes in working habits and relationships, that affects status and power, usually can come into effect only through a continued process of adjustment. The process may be long or short, easy or hard, successful or abortive, but all that the initial order can do is start the chain of action.

The subject of effectuating organizational changes is a fascinating one. I will not cover it systematically here, partly because of limitations of space and time, and partly because some useful studies of the subject have been recently published.[66]

But I do want to make some observations on some aspects of the subject which I feel have not had adequate attention or have been the subject of misinterpretation.[67]

A major fact to consider is the length of time often required for a sizeable reorganization, as indicated by the above passage from Professor Kaufman. Many people think of a reorganization as the formal announcement, with perhaps some time added for adjusting to the new plan. Actually, these form only a small part of a continuing process that includes at least the following stages:

1. Forces at work leading to the need for organizational change (technological, economic, personnel, program, legal, etc.).

2. Awareness of a problem (through complaints, disputes, poor results, etc.).

3. Analysis of the problem (may be short or extended).

4. Development of a solution (including consideration of alternatives).

5. The formal decision (which may be to do nothing). This stage includes an announcement of the change usually preceded by the grapevine. It is dangerous to concentrate attention on this stage only. Frequently the decision is in reality only a ratification of what has already happened informally. For example, actual decisions on purchase orders up to, say, $15,000 may have been made at a subordinate level for years before formal authority to do so is announced.

6. Implementation (working out of details, gaining acceptance and understanding).

7. Adjustments and evaluation of results (may take many years). Key questions are how long to wait before measuring results of the organizational changes made, and how to isolate the organizational changes as a causative factor from other changes occurring simultaneously.

Well before stage seven is reached, the cycle has started over again!

It is important to note that many, perhaps most, reorganizations do not take the form of official changes in the assignment of duties and responsibilities, or in the changing of boxes on the organization chart. Many real reorganizations are brought about in more subtle or indirect ways. For example, if a weak top executive is replaced by a strong one, the organization chart may stay the same, as may the formal distribution of duties and responsibilities, but in terms of decision–making and power centers the organization may operate in a considerably different manner. My guess is that there are more important organization changes brought about by the appointment of a particular type of person to a key executive job than by the formal reallocation of functions among different units.

To take another example, assume that a mistake is made by an official and that the mistake is attributed to his failure to clear with another unit. As a result, a directive is issued requiring certain clearances in all such cases in the future. Such a directive may not appear to be in the form of a reorganization, but it does change the balance of power and therefore the division of work.

The main reason why major changes in organization take so long to be effectuated is, as Herbert Kaufman well put it, because the status, power, and working habits of top executives are affected, and these are matters of emotion and anxiety. My own experience strongly supports this conclusion. I have discussed major reorganizations with key people affected some ten years after the formal change and found them still displaying deep emotions over the event. I have seen reorganizations explained to executives who had everything to gain and nothing to lose from the change, but whose initial impulse was to resist aggressively, largely because they felt such strong anxiety that they had not "heard" what was being said to them.

Perhaps the best known example of how hard it is to change accepted patterns through formal reorganization is the attempt since World War II to achieve unification of the armed forces.

Related to the question of how long it takes for the total reorganization process, are two questions of timing as they affect the formal change. One is the question of whether it is better to make a major reorganization in one fell swoop or as a series of separate actions. The second has to do with whether to announce and adopt the change as soon as it is decided on in principle, or to wait until all the details have been worked out.

Many people believe that too big a reorganization at one time is undesirable since it causes too much of a shock to be readily absorbed. I lean in the other direction, believing that a series of small reorganizations can frequently keep an enterprise in a state of turmoil where it might be better to "have done with it" so to speak. This feeling is perhaps based on my experience with the U. S. foreign aid program, where the constant changes from inside the State Department to outside and back again, plus the recurring changes in name and internal structure, have had an unfortunate effect on the morale and efficiency of the entire operation.[68]

Furthermore, there may be gains from a major organizational shake-up over and above the possible advantages of the new structure over the old. These gains arise from the opportunity which a major organizational change provides to bring new blood to the top, to "box-off" officials who no longer pull their weight, and to revitalize the thinking of key people.

On the second question, that of announcing and implementing the reorganization "sooner" or "later", the principal advantage of early action is to forestall rumors and anxiety; the principal advantages of later action are to be more certain that the decisions are basically sound and to avoid "tinkering" with the reorganized structure for undue periods of time. Frequently, here, it is feasible to announce the reorganization in principle, to be effective at a given future date (say three months hence), and at the same time to appoint a series of task forces to work out the details in advance of the effective date of reorganization.

The question of how to gain acceptance for major organizational changes is a perplexing one. Perhaps the most widely accepted generalization on this point is that "participation" on the part of those affected tends to minimize opposition to the changes to be made.[69] It is fairly well established that this can frequently be true with respect to procedural changes.[70] But I have some strong reservations with respect to the validity of this assumption for major organizational changes.

In the first place, the question depends on what kind of participation we are talking about. Participation in gathering relevant facts in the course of an organizational study is usually essential—if only to have at hand the data required to make intelligent decisions. But participation in reaching the decision is another matter. In almost any reorganization, someone gains in power and status—and someone loses. Thus, if the question is to assign a new function to A or B, one of them gets it and the other does not. Now if we should try to get A and B to agree on the best solution by getting their participation, we encounter the twin dangers of either the dominant person getting it, or of some compromise being reached that is a poorer solution than either one getting it. These dangers, it seems to me, more often than not outweigh the fact that they both might "accept" the solution with less resistance. On the other hand, if A and B merely give their views on the best solution, but don't go so far as to try to agree on one, then I think nothing has been gained in terms of getting acceptance from the one who does not benefit from the change.

A second reservation is that getting participation on the proposed solution frequently makes the proposal prematurely public. Thus, a proposed presidential reorganization plan, for example, if circulated for views among the departments concerned, would enable those departments which feel that they have been (or are likely to be) hurt to mobilize pressures among their interest groups and among congressmen who support them in time to help defeat the plan.

Similarly, many reorganization plans are developed by staff for presentation to the chief executive. Getting participation in advance may well upset numerous people if it turns out that the chief executive has no desire to adopt such a plan and the idea is dropped.

It is true that after the decision has been made by the chief executive to adopt a reorganization, even if only in general terms, participation in working out the details and in implementing the plan can well help achieve acceptance.

Crucial to the success of any formal reorganization is an appropriate and well thought out plan for implementation.[71] Such a plan should cover how the reorganization will be announced,[72] how the details will be worked out, and how follow-up will be maintained. The plan will have a better chance for success if the following points are kept in mind:

1. Of perhaps greatest importance is the willingness and ability of key executives to adapt themselves to the new plan. The chief executive must understand the new plan, believe in it, and consciously act within it rather than reverting to previous patterns. Key executives under him must change their behavior, as necessary, under the new plan. This is especially important, and difficult, where executives accustomed to line responsibility become central staff officers, as where the organization pattern has been changed from process or function to product or purpose.

2. There should be tolerance for some confusion for a short time after the formal change. The amount of confusion can be minimized if the implementation plan provides for adequate training, clear statements of responsibility, pilot installations, etc.

3. But top management must show that it means what it says. Sabotage cannot be tolerated. If people have been treated fairly rather than arbitrarily, top management has a right to insist that they give full support to the new plan.

4. One needs to face honestly the fact that in nearly all, if not all, major reorganizations, you can't have your cake and eat it. Some people gain and some people lose. Also, the gain to the enterprise (as in faster service, for example) is generally partially offset by some loss (as in less unformity). Some of the

greatest disillusionments I have seen over reorganizations arise when executives have been led to believe that the results will be all roses and no thorns.

5. Those responsible for follow–up of the reorganization should be on the lookout for unanticipated results—new alliances, new difficulties, new problems. The natural tendency is to look at *anticipated* benefits and problems. These frequently turn out not to be as crucial as the unforeseen developments.

By and large, I believe there has been too much emphasis on the problem of resistance to change. It is true that people resist change. It is also true that people welcome change. Many forces operate in both directions. The key is to enhance those forces supporting change and to minimize those opposing it. In any event, change is becoming more and more a way of life in any enterprise, and management must learn how to adjust to it as effectively as possible.[73]

In the jargon of the trade, the person with direct responsibility for the successful implementation of an organizational change is called the "change agent". The Foundation for Research on Human Behavior[74] has suggested the addition of a "change catalyst" to assist in major reorganizations. He would be an outsider without formal authority who would provide information and insights to assist the change agent. He would function by observing developments, predicting possible problems or tensions, testing his predictions, and making his findings available to help move the change along.

This raises the related question of the use of outside management consultants to plan, or help plan, new organizational patterns and, hopefully, to assist in their implementation. Such consultants may well be useful where an enterprise does not have qualified inside staff, or where there is such a staff but it doesn't have the time, or lacks the confidence of top management, or has a substantial vested interest in the outcome.

Even where there is a qualified internal staff with the time and top support, the use of outside consultants can frequently be valuable. Thus, such consultants can help gain acceptance for a new plan, as with a legislature or a board of directors. Also such consultants can take the brunt of the emotional reaction of those opposed to the change, thus leaving better future working relationships for the inside staff. (The penalty for taking responsibility for major reorganizations can be severe, as it was for James Forrestal, who reorganized the armed services, and Fowler Hamilton, who reorganized the Agency for International Development.)

It is also true, however, that an internal staff that is called on to develop a new organization plan can enhance its status and respect (but not necessarily its popularity) if the results are backed up by top management and are ultimately regarded as successful.

In this chapter, I have delved into some aspects of four perennial and perplexing organization problems. In the next chapter, I will cover some of the more common pitfalls facing the unwary organizer.

pitfalls and platitudes

There are many pitfalls that face the person concerned with a problem in organization.[75] Most of these pitfalls, I suppose, grow out of the understandable desire (even "need") to find an "easy" answer and to find the "right" answer. Unfortunately, because the problems are complex, easy answers are hard to come by; and because value systems differ and because the total environment of any enterprise is constantly in flux, right answers can only be relative to the person making the evaluation and to the time at which it is made.

Some of the pitfalls that I shall discuss appear in the form of platitudes—again as the result of the search for easy answers to complex problems.

PENDULUMITIS

One of the most common pitfalls may be referred to as "pendulumitis", otherwise known as "faddism". If one examines prevailing views about organization over a period of time, one gets the impression of a big overall pendulum together with many smaller pendulums, all swinging in one direction or another, and all swinging at different speeds and with different cycle times. When a particular pendulum is at one extreme, what it stands for often becomes dogma, articles of faith, and absolute truth for many people. Fortunately, it never stops at one extreme. Unfortunately, those who have swallowed uncritically all that it stands for tend to lag behind its return in their thinking. For any particular pendulum at any one time, it takes rigorous analysis to determine where it is in its path, and in which direction it is moving.

The overall pendulum takes the following form. Most of the early American writers in the field of organization were engineers who tended, consciously or unconsciously, to look at people in an enterprise as inanimate, just as they looked at machines and equipment. Their value system stressed efficiency, economy, productivity, and profits. The result was that they developed certain "universal prinicples" of organization based on the desire to routinize and control work. Then along came the "human relations" people with backgrounds in the social sciences. They stressed the fact that people are not machines but human beings with emotions, attitudes, feelings, and many needs besides security and safety. Their value system tended to stress democracy, equality, dignity of the individual, involvement, and the right of all employees to happiness and satisfaction in their work. The result was to question the validity of the previous "universal principles", or at least to change the emphasis from detailed division of work, routines, authority of the manager, strict controls, and formal organization, to participation, more interesting work (often through job enlargement), relaxed controls, informal organization and teamwork.

In recent years, the overall pendulum has swung back toward the middle. Harold J. Leavitt, for example, suggests that we are currently trying to achieve the best of both approaches: "to routinize and control what we can; to loosen up and make challenging what we cannot".[76]

In the same article, Mr. Leavitt notes with respect to the relationship between values and organization:

What shall we conclude? Using the common "efficiency" criteria, the Taylorists are right. But these are narrow and inhuman,
and if we use creativity and morale as criteria, modern participative beliefs are right. But are we also to conclude that the criteria of creativity and flexibility and morale are somehow
fundamentally more important than speed and clarity and order-
liness?

Or shall we (and I favor this conclusion) pragmatically conclude that if we want to achieve one kind of goal, then one kind
of structure seems feasible? If we want other criteria to govern,
then another structure may make sense. Certainly it is reasonable
to guess that in the real (as distinct from the laboratory) world,
there will be locations and times which might make one set of
criteria more important than the other even within the same
large organization.[77]

So much for the overall pendulum. There have also been
many interesting swings of the pendulum on particular aspects
of the organization problem. In the last couple of decades, for
example, many sweeping statements have been made about the
desirability of decentralization. Many writers have made decentralization a principle of organization; some have even
made it a fundamental task of management. But in recent
years, the pendulum has begun to swing back. Note, for
example, Louis A. Allen's article entitled "The Urge to Decentralize" in which he states: "Looking for a quick cure for
their organizational ills, many companies have found that a
fast dose of decentralization can do more harm than good."[78]
And, in the July, 1959, issue of *Dun's Review and Modern
Industry*, it is claimed that "hundreds of companies which
decentralized for growth during the post war boom years are
now, paradoxically, recentralizing—again for growth".[79] The
major reasons are said to be too much decentralization too
soon, costly errors at the division level, new central staff groups
in such fields as long–range planning and research and development, and the adoption of computers. Along the same lines,
John Dearden says in a recent issue of the *Harvard Business*

Review: "For many companies, profit decentralization is the *worst* possible answer".[80]

The real issue is, should we at this time further centralize or further decentralize (it's all a matter of degree) in our own unique circumstances? As a matter of fact, it might well be that we should further centralize some activities and further decentralize others at the same time.

Other examples of "pendulumitis" come readily to mind. Thus, early writers on organization said categorically that the span of control should not be more than five or six. Then the reaction set in and businesses such as Sears Roebuck & Company and others vastly increased the span of control, maintaining that this freed their managers from too close supervision, thus enabling them to develop with more freedom and to be more clearly held accountable. Now we say that the span of control might be large, medium, or small depending on many different circumstances.

Until recent years, specialization and the assembly line were fixed attributes of efficient production in the minds of most people. Then it became fashionable to attribute worker dissatisfaction to monotony and boredom brought about by specialization. This led to a plea for something called "job enlargement" to give each individual a greater variety of tasks to do. Currently, a carefully reasoned article[81] points out that most workers, even in routine jobs are not dissatisfied; that what dissatisfaction does exist is largely the result of factors other than specialization; that many people prefer routine work; and that the problem is largely in the eyes of the beholder, not the worker. ("The observer says to himself, 'That job would drive me nuts in half an hour.' From this he somehow concludes that it must drive everyone else nuts as well. This simply is not so!")[82]

The principal and most basic tool of the early organizers was the organization chart. Along came the sophisticates who, realizing the limitations of the chart in that it could not show the informal organization, prided themselves on not allowing an organization chart in the place. Again the pendulum swings, and organization charts are back in style. This time their limitations are recognized, but their value in forcing certain organization problems to be thought through and in gaining understanding for the formal relationships in the enterprise is appreciated.[83]

Not so long ago, managers and recruiters looked for the man who could fit easily into an enterprise—who had tact, who could work with others, and who conformed to the mores of the company or agency. The pendulum is now (at least in theory, if not in practice) at the other extreme where we look for the creative and innovative man and abhor the conformist. The pendulum will swing back, but probably not all the way. One should remember that he also serves who does a good, sound job, even if it is not new and different.

Even within the field of human relations and human motivation, we find the same ebb and flow. We can consider ourselves relatively modern if we accept concepts of democratic administration, participative management and the bottom–up approach. Yet in a recent issue of the *Harvard Business Review*, Robert N. McMurry discards the validity and practical nature of these concepts and makes a plea for "benevolent autocracy" in the management of business enterprise.[84] Donald R. Schoen in the preceding issue of the same journal also took a hard look at some of these human relations fads in an article entitled "Human Relations: Boon or Bogle?"[85]

There are many other examples of pendulumitis in other related fields of management. Thus, it is currently fashionable to attack the use and value of psychological testing[86] and to question the traditional approach to handling personnel appraisals.[87] It is my guess that within a decade, both psychological tests and performance appraisals will be back in favor as essential tools of management.

What happens so often, I believe, is that the creator of an idea or concept hedges it carefully with appropriate qualifications and limitations. Then, gradually, his disciples accept the major thesis as dogma, dropping all else. This leaves the proposition in its extreme or, perhaps, oversimplified form, easily subject to attack by those who, from whatever motivation, wish to take the opposite side of the question. The reaction, in turn and in time, assumes its own extreme form, leading to counter-reaction, and so the process goes on.

Before leaving the subject of "pendulumitis" or "faddism", I would like to identify two sub–categories. The first, I call "majority rule". This is where one discovers (from some survey) that 62 per cent of the companies with between 5,000 and 7,500 employees in his industry have established separate community relations departments, so he decides that he must have one; or that twelve companies in the past year combined organization planning with executive development, so it must be a good idea. Often such surveys, upon analysis, turn out to be based on the flimsiest of premises and field work, and often the conclusions seem only distantly related to the data.

The second has to do with the need of those making an organization study to make a contribution. I can illustrate this point with an apocryphal story that used to be told around the U.S. Bureau of the Budget. The story goes that in making a study of a federal agency, the bureau was about to recommend that it adopt a strong executive type of organization. It then discovered that the agency already had a strong executive type organization, so it was forced to recommend the adoption of a weak executive type!

Fads change, the pendulum swings, the bandwagon rolls on. If one organizes by fad alone, he will be out of step within a few years. Therefore, he is better advised to organize to meet his own needs, not someone else's philosophy, even if that philosophy expresses the "truth" of the day.

DOCTRINAIRISM

A second, and closely related, pitfall is "doctrinairism" (referred to by some as "sloganitis"). "We have abolished all assistants", says one agency or company. "We never use committees", says another. "Our line units only operate and our staff units only advise", says a third. Now if these policies are slavishly followed in any sizeable enterprise, then I would think that the enterprise is paying extreme penalties for a contrived and artificial approach. But I don't believe for a moment that they are adopted literally and completely. Close investigation, I am convinced, will usually show that these statements are merely slogans of the top man (or more likely those of one of his staff assistants). Scratch beneath the surface and you discover that there are committees but they are called "task forces" or "study groups"; there are assistants but they are called "secretaries", "technicians", or you name it; and inevitably line units use the staff techniques of advice and persuasion, and staff units not only advise but operate and control—though perhaps under the fiction that they do so only in the name of their boss.

A typical doctrinaire statement frequently made in government circles is that positions are classified on the basis of duties and responsibilities without reference to the person holding the job. Yet it is common knowledge that the words used in the job description (as distinguished from the actual work done) frequently affect the classification, and that many "reorganizations" are made principally for the purpose of getting some one person a higher grade. There are many ways to beat the system. Here is a typical example of how it works in practice. The U.S. Operations [technical assistance] Mission to an underdeveloped country requested that headquarters recruit a budget advisor to assist the country in revising its budget system. The country and the U.S. mission had a particular person in mind. The duties and responsibilities of the job were written up and sent to Washington. The headquarters personnel office classified the job at a level which turned out to be too low to attract the individual desired. Whereupon the program people in Washington cabled the field mission this fact and added, "Please review the duties and responsibilities of the job as submitted and see if they have changed".

Two additional observations on doctrinairism are pertinent.

For one thing, doctrinairism seems to affect the "verbal" system much more severely than the "operational" system. Many a manager who expresses fixed and dogmatic views on organization (usually explaining his behavior in terms of traditional and orthodox "principles"), actually operates in a much more flexible and realistic way. Thus the practical effects are not as severe as they might seem. Secondly, since doctrinaire views, like principles and proverbs, tend to occur in opposite pairs (DuPont loves committees; General Electric wouldn't be caught dead with one), it is possible to select either view with the comforting knowledge that there is support for your position.

My antidote for doctrinairism, as must be apparent from the previous chapters, is pragmatism—doing what works with due regard to both the long–run and short–run interests of the enterprise.

OVERSIMPLIFICATION

A third pitfall is oversimplification. If my experience has taught me anything, it is that the "192 principles" of organization that can be extracted from the textbooks do not begin to answer even the *least* complex organization problems. Why? There are many reasons. Values differ, conditions change, all the facts are rarely (if ever) available, non–rational as well as rational factors influence the decisions made. But the most pervasive reason is that organizing involves people. And people react on the basis of an almost infinite number of stimuli. I have yet to participate in the discussion of a concrete organization problem in which we did not spend more time discussing how a key figure would react, and the abilities, prejudices, likes and dislikes, and strengths and weaknesses of the principal executives involved than all the time (if any) spent discussing "unity of command", "span of control", the "scalar principle", and the "general staff concept".

Let's take the simplest kind of an organization problem as an example. Assume that the XYZ Bureau is organized as in Figure 12.

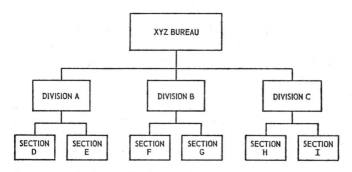

FIGURE 12. ORGANIZATION CHART OF THE XYZ BUREAU

Assume that the head of Division A leaves the agency and the question arises as to whether to replace him (thus continuing the same organization structure) or to abolish the position and raise Sections D and E to division level. What are the important considerations here?

A review of the traditional principles of organization fails to turn up any that are of particular help in solving this problem.

There are some rational, albeit rather mechanical, guides that can be used. For example, one would want to consider how much money, if any, would be saved by abolishing Division A; a comparison of Sections D and E with Divisions B and C in terms of size of staff, size of budget, importance of work and complexity of work; and the amount of time available to the bureau chief to supervise directly the work of Sections D and E if they were made divisions.

But other unique and personal factors would unquestionably be more important. For example, if one of the section heads of Section D or E was senior in experience and clearly superior in ability, he would expect to be promoted to chief of

Division A; if both were highly qualified and potential top executives, there would be a tendency to abolish Division A and create two new divisions making both persons division chiefs; but if neither was qualified for advancement, an outsider would probably be brought in to head Division A. Other important considerations would be the capacities and style of operation of the bureau chief, the reactions of the chiefs of Divisions B and C to raising Sections D and E to division level, and the reactions of the chiefs of Sections F, G, H, and I to such a move.

Two special forms of oversimplification deserve mention. One is the "panacea" fallacy. This holds that a reorganization, for example, will solve all problems; that it will be all things to all people. It can't and it won't. A reorganization may result in certain advantages (e.g., improved morale or better productivity), but it will inevitably entail certain disadvantages (e.g., new conflicts, greater costs, etc.). Frequently the disadvantages of any existing organization plan and the presumed advantages of a prospective plan seem to show up most clearly. In other words, far fields look green. It is only after a reorganization, that the disadvantages of the new plan become crystal clear. One can only plan for the net effect to be advantageous in terms of his own interpretation of the objectives of the enterprise. It should also be noted that a change in organization will not ordinarily solve problems that have their roots elsewhere (e.g., unclear objectives, incompetent leadership, inadequate funds, political interference, or lack of public support). I might pause to note, also, that measuring the results of a reorganization can be extremely difficult due principally to the many other factors simultaneously at work. Measuring the results of *not* reorganizing is probably even more difficult.

A second type of oversimplification, affecting the literal–minded, is preoccupation with the quantitative approach. Since intangibles are subjective, these people focus attention on things that can be measured, and attempt to derive organization decisions from countable factors: the size of each unit, the number of subordinates reporting to each supervisor, the number of decisions made by each manager, the amount of work produced, etc. The quantitative approach gives an aura of objectivity to the study of organization, but in the present stage of our ability to measure, it covers only a small fraction of the factors affecting important organization decisions, ignoring such important considerations as informal relationships, communication patterns, leadership styles, and management climate. While these factors may not be countable, they do "count" when it comes to organizing. I have seen the quantitative approach used where it appeared obvious to me that the problem was oversimplified and distorted to fit a convenient mathematical formula, rather than developing a formula that would fit the real problem.

PASSION FOR PLANNING

A fourth pitfall, a passion for planning, is a danger that even some of the most brilliant organizers seem unable to avoid. This pitfall is characterized by the drafting of beautiful plans —period. The real challenge to the organization planner is not in developing an improved organization plan. Difficult though that may be, it is child's play compared to the problems of how to gain acceptance for the plan and how to make it work. Since I have discussed some of these problems earlier[88] I need not go into them again at this point.

Unless this pitfall is avoided, one of two things can happen. Either the plan never gets adopted, or if it is adopted, it runs into so many difficulties that it is either formally or informally discarded.

Even in those instances when a new plan is in operation and working satisfactorily, there may well remain an additional problem. Those who think only in terms of preparing an ideal organization plan tend not to think of organizing as a continuing process. They tend to regard their masterpiece as something that will last, if not for the millennium, at least for a lifetime. This introduces an inflexibility into organizing that is dangerous.

Moreover, those persons who become enamored of planning seem also to be those who search for (and therefore "find") universals that are supposedly applicable to *all* situations for *all* people for *all* times. The plan becomes an end in itself, rather than a means to accomplish certain results. And if the results are poor, it can't be because the plan isn't suitable, but because the "stupid" people in the particular agency or company can not or will not fit into it properly. After all, since the plan is "rational" and "logical", the people must be "irrational", "illogical", "prima donnas", "personality problems", or, at best, "incompetents".

Economy / Efficiency Cult

The next pitfall I wish to cover is the belief that organizational decisions are entirely or principally aimed at achieving economy and efficiency. I am using these terms here in their narrow sense of saving money, increasing productivity, and improving service as distinguished from effectiveness, which may be defined as meeting the long–run objectives of the enterprise. An example may help explain the difference. If an agency established a district office in the home town of the chairman of the appropriations subcommittee which handles its budget not because there is need for the office from a management point of view but only to satisfy this congressman, then economy and efficiency are not being achieved, although the net result might be that the agency will be able to function more effectively.

A leading, experienced organization planner in private industry has told me that he knows of only four circumstances under which major reorganizations have been adopted. These are:

1. Change in objectives.
2. Change in the chief executive.
3. Economic necessity.
4. Drastic changes in volume.

If this observation is accurate, then efficiency and economy are not the only reasons for organizational change in business. The same would appear to be true in government based on the study of eleven cases of reorganization which I have already mentioned.[89] In these cases, efficiency / economy was found to be only one of ten goals of reorganization. While nearly always *stated* as one purpose of the reorganization, this purpose was usually not significant.[90] The other nine goals were:

1. To facilitate expansion of a program.
2. To change program emphasis.
3. To enlarge or protect the power of a top executive or group within the agency.
4. To respond to or satisfy outside threats or criticism.
5. To achieve order, rationality, or symmetry.
6. To correct personnel problems (e.g., to "box off" one or more executives, or conversely to advance one or more executives more rapidly).
7. To increase morale, as by providing opportunities for advancement.
8. To scuttle an organization unit or a program.
9. To bring about change for its own sake (as when new leadership wants to shake things up).[91]

It is not only true that many organizational changes are made principally for reasons other than efficiency and economy. It is also true that many organizational changes that would have achieved efficiency and economy are *not* made for various other reasons.

As noted earlier, changes in organization have a real impact on people (particularly executives) in terms of power, status, and their general psyche. Changes in organization can also have profound influence on policies and programs. Let's take a few examples.

Prior to 1953, the U. S. technical assistance program was handled largely by the Technical Cooperation Administration (TCA), a semi-independent part of the State Department. The leaders of this agency firmly believed in the technical assistance program as a long–range, small–cost program to help the underdeveloped countries to help themselves on the road to a higher standard of living. When it was proposed to combine TCA with the Mutual Security Administration (MSA), which handled economic aid and military aid in addition to technical assistance to some countries, into a single new independent agency (this was later to become the Foreign Operations Administration), there was strong and emotional resistance on the part of the TCA officials. They felt that such a combination would subordinate the long–range goals of the technical assistance program to short–range U. S. foreign policy needs and cause some neutralist countries to refuse technical assistance because of the strings that would inevitably be attached. Of course, integrating the technical assistance program more closely into our total mutual security program was one of the principal reasons that the proponents advanced in favor of the consolidation.

Another example in the technical assistance field is the battle that was waged as to whether the agency handling this program should be a small coordinating agency using various existing departments (Department of Agriculture, Office of Education, Public Health Service, etc.) to handle this work, or a strong agency itself providing assistance in these fields. The principal arguments made were: a weak central agency with the actual work being done by existing agencies would cause difficult coordination problems and would reduce the effectiveness of the technical assistance program since the existing agencies would undoubtedly apply their best skills and energies to domestic problems, giving only the time and attention not so required to the foreign activities; a strong central agency would have the drive and incentive to carry out its program aggressively but would be expensive because it would duplicate skills available elsewhere in the government and might compete with domestically-oriented agencies for skilled personnel already in short supply. The fundamental question was over the kind of foreign aid program that was desired rather than the most efficient or economical method of operation.

Another example, familiar to most students of public administration, can be found in the organizational location of the personnel function. The traditional central, independent civil service commission was created to exercise certain control functions, notably prevention of the employment of friends, relatives, or party adherents at the expense of employment on the basis of merit. It was made independent to insure its integrity as a watchdog over the executive. This is a laudable goal. Nevertheless, many now feel that a central personnel agency ought to be a part of the chief executive's staff (rather than independent) in order to put more emphasis on what has been called "positive" personnel administration, that is, those aspects of the function dealing with personnel program formulation and administration including development of people, motivation, human relations, etc. In other words, the organizational decision affects the policy—whether emphasis is to be put on keeping the "bad guys" out, or whether it is to be put on getting the "good guys" in.

President Franklin D. Roosevelt is generally regarded as having been a poor administrator, partly because he created new agencies to perform functions closely related to those already being performed by existing agencies. This might have been costly in the immediate sense. But President Roosevelt clearly understood that to give the emphasis he wanted to certain programs, the creation of a new agency with new executives and unencumbered by past precedents and years of red tape was the best way to accomplish his objectives. On this score, at least, I give him high marks as a top-notch administrator.

Herbert A. Simon provides us with another example of the effects of organization on program in his account of the creation of the Economic Cooperation Administration:

. . . reorganization can seldom affect efficiency without affecting program goals. When we change the organization, we change the picture that the people in it have of the concrete task to be done and the concrete goals to be achieved—their concept of the program. When we change the concept of the program we change the relative emphasis that the various parts of the complex whole will receive, we alter allocations of resources and relative priorities among goals.[92]

On the other hand, it is undoubtedly true that there are some cases where major changes in organization have not significantly affected policy (and probably not efficiency and economy either). Francis E. Rourke, for example, points out in a case study of one such reorganization,[93]

The shift of the Bureau of Employment Security from the Federal Security Agency to the Department of Labor proved to be of little more significance than a change of address. . . . Predominant power over the formulation of national employment security policy continued to rest with the coalition of state agencies and employer groups as it had in the past. The influence exercised by these interest groups over the employment security program proved to be based on something considerably more substantial than a particular organizational arrangement or the degree of sympathy for their point of view felt by national administrative officials.[94]

My own view, however, is that such cases are relatively rare, and that major organizational changes, more often than not, do have an important impact on policies and programs as well as on efficiency and economy.[95] A somewhat different problem that also arises with those who overstress efficiency and economy is that they fail to ask the question, "efficiency and economy for whom and for what?" The establishment of a centralized purchasing system, for example, will usually save money on the cost of purchases for the enterprise as a whole, provide equipment and supplies of generally higher quality, lower inventory levels, and help insure against favoritism in purchasing. But from the point of view of the operating unit which formerly did its own purchasing, the result may well be delays in the provision of needed supplies and materials, increased paperwork and follow–up, and possibly being required to use uniform items (to achieve economies in large–scale purchasing) most suitable to the organization as a whole, but not best suited to that particular unit's needs. Similarly, decentralization of engineering to operating units might well result in structures being completed at an earlier date and at lower costs, but with the penalty of lower quality work and added risks with respect to the durability or integrity of the structure.

One might pause to wonder whether an agency, or company, that was operating with "perfect" efficiency and economy today would be best adapted to change in order to meet the new circumstances of tomorrow. Perhaps, in reality, such a situation would lead to complacency, to self–satisfaction and to emphasis on today's problems. A little disorderliness, a little confusion, a little waste and a little discord might provide more incentive to change and improve, and thus permit more ready adaptability to new circumstances. As a matter of fact, recent research on the subject of creativity seems to show that the creative person thrives on disorder, and responds to it by constructing new and superior arrangements. For him, disorder is a powerful motivating force.

Perhaps it is academic even to discuss the possibility of "perfect" order. While it appears to be true that man has a need to create order out of disorder, it is probably equally true that he will strive to create disorder out of order. As someone has said, "Man, the problem solver, is even more man, the problem maker".

Fortunately, those who take the narrow "efficiency and economy" view are most likely to be specialists in organization planning. The result can be very frustrating for them. However, most top executives are well aware of the personal, program, and policy implications involved in major organization changes, and make their decisions accordingly.

CONFLICT–PHOBIA

Another common pitfall may be referred to as "conflict–phobia"—a fear of conflict, or a belief that an organization is healthy when things are running smoothly without friction or open differences of opinion.[96]

Quite to the contrary, I believe that conflict, in the sense of bringing to bear differing points of view on a problem, ought to be accepted, even encouraged, and out in the open so that decisions can be made based on consideration of all relevant views. In a new organization, or one which is changing rapidly, it is particularly important to organize in such a way that conflicts are not resolved or concealed at too low a level; that disagreements are sharpened and defined so that policy decisions can be made consciously by top management for future guidance of all executives of the enterprise.

The Port of New York Authority offers a good example. On the one hand, the Authority must be self–supporting and therefore has to be net revenue conscious; on the other, its function is to provide service to the public of the Port District in the field of transportation and transportation terminals. These two objectives may sometimes be in conflict with each other. To insure that where they are, the decision gets made at the proper level, we have so organized that our line (or operating) departments are primarily responsible for seeing that our facilities pay for themselves. But our staff departments, particularly our Port Development and our Operations Services Departments, are concerned principally with the goal of providing adequate public service. When there is disagreement between a line department and the Port Development or Operations Services Department, the problem is carried to a higher level for resolution.

Some types of conflict are undoubtedly undesirable. The Port Authority's Administrative Manual tries to distinguish between those which are desirable and those which are not as follows:

To the extent that conflicts and disagreements between organization units sharpen issues for decision at the next higher level and are reasonable expressions of differing ideas on how best to accomplish a common purpose, they are desirable; they are undesirable when they arise from personality conflicts, preoccupation with personal or jurisdictional status, confused allocation of responsibilities, or similar causes which tend to divide the staff and lead to antagonisms.

Management's task is to foster and support conflict of the first type, while holding to a minimum conflict of the second. This it does by such methods as building a common loyalty to the organization and its objectives, but not to particular solutions; establishing a climate that welcomes and rewards new ideas; promoting the problem–solving approach rather than the precedent–following approach; organizing in such a way as to insure a fair hearing for varying points of view; and fostering an attitude concerning differing views that goes beyond trying to determine which is "right" to trying to determine how and why each view developed as it did.

Where tranquility, harmony, and general agreement are regarded as "good" and their opposites as "bad", there is a climate established which inhibits vigor, vitality and involvement, and may prevent the restless, and perhaps irritating, individualist from expressing a "different" or even "revolutionary" idea. But this might be just the idea that will help the enterprise meet developing changes in the environment not yet perceived by those happy and contented individuals who are more interested in getting along well with their fellow workers, or in avoiding any appearance of emotional upset or dissatisfaction.

Any enterprise in which open and admitted differing points of view and conflict did not appear would seem to be either (1) complacent, self–satisfied, and therefore unlikely to progress; or (2) smothering problems at low levels in the structure so that they smoulder unnoticed by top management until real trouble flares; or (3) one in which certain interests are dominated by others to such an extent that the weaker groups fear to express themselves resulting ultimately in decisions based on inadequate data, as well as apathy and poor motivation on the part of those who could not or would not be heard.

The Total Systems Approach

Another pitfall, of relatively recent origin, is known as the "total systems approach".[97] As applied to organization it would go something like this. Assume a bureau with three divisions (see Fig. 13). Since the work of Division A is undoubtedly related in some way to the work of Divisions B and C (since all are in the same bureau), the organization of Division A should not be studied without taking into account the effect of any possible changes on the rest of the bureau, thus requiring a study and possible reorganization of the entire bureau.

In many cases this interrelationship is a valid consideration, and must be kept in mind by the person or persons developing a reorganization plan for Division A. However, there are many cautions. In the first place, there may be reasons why Divisions B and C are not ready to accept any reorganization. Should this stop a reorganization of Division A? Yes, if a reorganization of Division A would significantly hamper the work of the other Divisions. No, if the reorganization would help Division A but

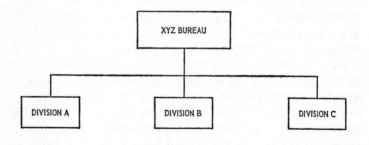

FIGURE 13. XYZ BUREAU

would not adversely affect the work of Divisions B and C in any major way, even though the result would not be as complete a job as a total reorganization.

In the second place, if Division A could not be studied or reorganized without considering the organization of the entire bureau, this might inhibit innovation and experimentation on the part of the management of Division A, partly because the overall job might be just too big to undertake, and partly because it would not have the authority to do the entire job. To take an analogy in the technological field, it is very possible that "hi–fi" record players would not be as good as they are if each component (speaker, tuner, amplifier, and turntable) had been developed in relation to precise overall specifications set by a single manufacturer rather than being developed by independent manufacturers with no central control and supervision. The reason, again, is that the attempt to fit each component into a preconceived plan might have reduced innovations adopted when working separately.

I have heard conservative business men advocate the total systems approach without realizing that they were coming close to supporting totalitarianism, or at least overall economic planning. The same business men profess to believe in the advantages of a system of free enterprise which allows individual firms in the economy to make their own decisions unrelated to any controlling total system.

In the third place, if we take "total systems" literally, then it should be noted that the XYZ Bureau is related to other bureaus in the same department, that this department is related to other departments in the same government, leading us to the conclusion that no reorganization can be made unless it is of the government as a whole! And if this were the federal government, it should not, following the same reasoning, be studied or reorganized without considering the whole federal system in all its dimensions including states and municipalities, not to mention the United Nations and the governments of other national states! One of the difficulties of this approach is graphically portrayed by one of my friends who said: "Long before I ever heard of the total systems approach, I always took into account all the factors *I knew how to*".

I was once associated with an organization planner who eventually had to be replaced—not because he couldn't see the forest for the trees, but because he couldn't see the trees for the forest. If assigned to a study of the organization of the central files operation, for example, a job that might have taken one or two months, he would return a year later with a plan for reorganizing the entire agency. Whatever the assignment, the answer was always the same. Each step led naturally to the next. And perhaps the proposed overall reorganization had merit. However, the top management of the agency had no desire to reorganize and saw no problems significant enough to warrant such a step. As a result, the specific unit that would have benefited from organizational changes stayed the same.

What I sometimes think proponents of the total systems approach are *really* saying is that if you have a small problem you cannot solve, by making it bigger you have a better excuse for not solving it.

It is likely that the total systems approach to organization would be more appropriate when designing the organization for a new enterprise than when reorganizing a going concern. Even here, however, there are cautions. A new enterprise might not be as "new" as it first appears. Thus, one of the newest federal agencies, the National Aeronautics and Space Administration (NASA), was basically created by the transfer to it of other federal units such as the National Advisory Committee for Aeronautics, The Vanguard and Upper Atmosphere Groups of the Office of Naval Research, the Jet Propulsion Laboratory of the Ordnance Corps of the Department of the Army, and the Development Operations Division of the Army Ballistic Missiles Agency. Each of these units had its own culture and its own way of operating. It was extremely difficult to change these patterns from any overall, "total systems" point of view.

Another new agency, The Peace Corps, escaped this problem

to a large degree in its creation as an almost wholly new and separate enterprise. Had it been made a part of the foreign aid agency (now Agency for International Development) as originally contemplated, it would have had much less freedom in adopting organizational and management patterns suitable to its own needs. In other words, a sub–system (The Peace Corps) could be organized effectively without reference to the "total" system (all U.S. foreign operations?). Rationalizing the total program of foreign operations might at first appear to be the most logical approach. But from a practical point of view, it might well have meant bogging The Peace Corps down with the same impediments that have been so hard to remove from the rest of the foreign aid program.

In sum, solutions to the "total" organization problems of an enterprise, even where "logically" desirable may often be impracticable. A series of improvements in the organization of sub–systems of the enterprise may often get greater results in a given period of time.[98] It seems to me that, in most cases, trying to change a "total system" to meet fast–changing situations would be much more difficult and unwieldly than making changes in various elements of the system.

In any event, the concept of "total systems" implies "total solutions". The concept of "total solutions" implies "right solutions", and as I have pointed out, there are no "right solutions" except in relation to given values and these vary by culture, by individual and over time. In fact, I know of no "total solution" short of "total annihilation".

AESTHETICS

The next pitfall has to do with "aesthetics", or the tendency to make an organizational virtue of symmetry, balance, and uniformity.

A typical example is reflected in the military table of organization. An infantry company is supposed to have the same number of people in each category regardless of the ability of its personnel or of differences in the functions it happens to be performing at the time. The results in practice, however, are not so bad. If an extra man is needed in the supply room to help the supply sergeant, he is taken out of the mess hall or out of a rifle squad and put into the supply room. When the inspectors come around, he returns to his formally assigned post; when they leave, he returns to where he is needed.

Similarly, if one line department has three staff divisions of its own, those who succumb to this pitfall feel that all line departments must have the same. Or if a central staff engineering department handles construction work for one line department, they believe that it should handle construction for all line departments, even though the nature of the construction may vary considerably.

Some of the best–known authorities in the field of organization have stated that a basic principle of organization is that the organization should be "in balance". I'm not sure exactly what this means. Certainly, I can think of many cases where the organization should be purposely out of balance. Thus if one particular program or function is of critical importance at a particular time, then it should undoubtedly be given special support.

And I have heard organization planners considering a proposed change in organization raise objections because the organization *chart* is not symmetrical. Of what possible relevance this is to the desirability of adopting the proposed plan, I completely fail to see.

COMMUNICATIONS

The last of the pitfalls I wish to mention is the belief that communications follow the chain of command. Even those who are sufficiently enlightened to believe in communications as a two–way process (i.e., that managers should listen to their subordinates as well as talking to or at them) frequently fall into this trap.

To my mind, the basic communications problem in an enterprise is not communications from management to employee (by way of such devices as bulletin boards, employee newspapers, staff meetings, instructions and the like); nor is it communications from employee to management (by way of such devices as reports, attitude surveys, suggestion systems, staff meetings and the like). The significant problem is communications between and among all employees in the course of getting the work done on a day by day basis.

It follows that most communications (other than such things as orders and reports) should travel horizontally and diagonally as well as vertically. Information needed in the process of doing the work of an agency should ordinarily flow in the simplest and most direct way practicable. This means that one should directly contact the person who has the information he needs, or who needs the information he has, without going through middlemen.

There are, of course, some common–sense qualifications to this approach, as follows:

1. Where more than one person may be able to supply the needed information, it should ordinarily be obtained from the person nearest the requestor's own horizontal level.

2. If the requestor has reason to believe that his own supervisor, or one of his colleagues, may have already obtained the information, he should check within his own unit before going outside.

3. In making contacts outside one's own unit, an employee should keep his supervisor promptly informed as to:

a. matters for which he (the supervisor) may be held accountable to *his* supervisor;

b. matters which may result in misunderstandings with the other unit; and

c. matters which involve possible changes in established policies.[99]

I might also add that many of those who are promoting the idea of communications as a "two–way" process make two other assumptions which I think will not stand up. One is that "the more communications the better". It would seem to me that there is an "optimum" amount of communications that falls somewhere between the maximum and minimum, depending on the situation. The problem is the quality, effectiveness and relevance of the communications, not the quantity of communications.

The second assumption is that communications takes place only between and among people. A growing problem in modern, large enterprises is that of communications between man and machine, and between machine and machine. A whole new set of criteria will have to be developed to govern communications of these two new types.[100]

There are undoubtedly many other pitfalls facing unwary managers in the field of organization, as there are platitudes adopted by them. Those that I have mentioned are the ones that I have run into most frequently.

There is an inherent pitfall in constructing any list of pitfalls. This is the danger of making each pitfall a straw man, and then going to the other extreme in attempting to demolish it. Whether I have fallen into this trap, the reader will have to decide for himself.

FIVE

prospects and prophecies

Someone with a wry sense of humor once noted that there is nothing more difficult to predict than—the future. Trying to forecast what lies ahead in the field of organization is especially hazardous for one who, like myself, believes that the present state of the "art" permits precious few valid generalizations.

Three things I can say with confidence. These are that the environment will change; that our values will change; and that as our environment and our values change, organizational concepts, patterns, and practices will change. As for the precise nature of these changes, no one (except the novice) can be sure.

This "law of uncertainty" (not to be confused with a law of similar name as used by physicists) does not absolve the student in any field from at least speculating about the shape of the future. This I will do by reviewing some of the major social and technological factors that are most likely to affect organization in the future and by making some "educated" guesses as to how. It is probable that some of these different social and technological developments will have opposite effects on organization (e.g., some tending to push in the direction of decentralization, others in the direction of centralization).

Where there are important countervailing forces, the net effect may be in one direction or the other, or even, if the forces are approximately equal, in no discernible direction at all.

SIZE OF THE ENTERPRISE

One of the clearest trends over the past few decades is the growth in size of individual government agencies (federal, state or local) and private companies.[101] A glance at the federal budget past and present for most federal agencies demonstrates this growth in the government. Comparing expenditures for three typical agencies in 1940 and 1964 shows the Department of Justice increasing from $52.6 million to $328.0 million, the Post Office Department from $42.0 million to $578.0 million, and the Interstate Commerce Commission from $8.8 million to $24.4 million. Even allowing for changes in the value of the dollar, these are substantial increases. And as is well–known today, state and local governments are growing at a far faster rate than the federal government.

Similarly, a comparison of the present size of the largest companies in the United States with the size of the largest companies twenty or thirty years ago will show the same trend. Using gross sales as a measure, for example, in 1939 only two companies exceeded $1 billion (largest, $1.4 billion); by 1949, seventeen companies exceeded this figure (largest, $5.7 billion); by 1960, some forty-nine companies exceeded the same volume of sales (largest, $12.7 billion), and by 1964, over sixty-seven companies exceeded $1 billion in sales (largest, $17.0 billion).[102] Again, these increases far exceed those due to change in the value of the dollar.

In my judgment, this trend will continue. One reason, affecting both government and industry, is Parkinson's Law—too familiar by now to need to be spelled out.[103] Other reasons are growing population—in urban areas, in the country as a whole, and in the world; changed technology which makes larger units more efficient for technical and financial reasons; and improved methods of communication and transportation which make large enterprises workable.

Government agencies will continue to grow simply because the overall role of government is becoming bigger in our society, and the problems faced by government are becoming more complex and more important to survival. Also, the services demanded by an increasingly affluent society become greater in quantity and quality. For example, the journey to work for an employee a hundred years ago required two legs, or possibly a horse and buggy. Today it takes a bus, highway, planning board, bus station, public service commission, gas stations, unions, and congressional investigations—to mention only a few of the "necessities".

Business also will continue to grow as international activities are added, as mergers are undertaken to achieve economies and to utilize scarce resources more effectively, and as additional resources become needed to handle complex activities growing out of increased knowledge and more sophisticated technology.

Moreover, there is a circular effect (vicious, or not, depending on the point of view) resulting from the concentration of power in any one sector. Thus, big business tends to necessitate big government and vice versa; not to mention big unions and other big institutions that are both a result and a cause of big business and big government.

What are the implications for organization of this growth in the size of individual enterprises? Principally, I think, the very fact that agencies and companies are becoming larger will be a powerful force toward further decentralization within the enterprise. This is simply because the larger the organization, the more difficult it becomes to do everything at the top.

I should like to note, however, that increased size, *looked at from the point of view of the overall economy*, will result in a degree of centralization. Thus, Company XYZ, with two divisions, A and B, may buy three new companies C, D, and E and set them up as Divisions C, D, and E. Since *some* of the decisions formerly made by the president or board of directors of Companies C, D and E are now made by the president or board of XYZ, this must be construed as centralization. However, *from the point of view of Company XYZ itself*, its top management, with a much larger company to run, can usually not make all the operating, and even policy, decisions it formerly made, and will probably delegate some of them to Divisions A, B, C, D and E. This, of course, would be decentralization.

One might well ask why any of the decisions formerly made by C, D and E when they were separate companies, should need to be made above the division level in the new company. There are several answers. One reason would be to insure that the policies of those at the top are adopted by the various divisions. This can be a real problem when it means changing the direction of thinking of a formerly independent entity. I well remember the difficulty the Technical Cooperation Administration had when it took over the Institute of Inter–American Affairs in trying to broaden the approach of the latter beyond its traditional, and successful, programs in health, agriculture and education into other fields (such as industry and public administration), and beyond the single device of the "servicio",[104] or joint operation. Other reasons are to insure the optimum allocation of resources among the different divisions, and to insure that each division is acting in the overall interest of the company as a whole rather than in its own individual interest.

While decentralization would seem to be a natural result of increasing size, we have had enough experience with unsuccessful, or only partially successful, attempts at decentralization to be fairly certain that there will have to be an accompanying trend, and that is the development of better ways by which top management, having decentralized, can keep abreast of what is going on. Therefore in the future I look for considerably more attention to this problem of developing new and more effective controls as a necessary prerequisite for further decentralization. In other words, the future might well see more centralized controls simultaneously with more decentralized functions.

Evidence pointing to the impact of size on organization can be found in a recent report of the National Industrial Conference Board in which Harold Stieglitz identified four emerging trends in the organization of business concerns.[105] A principal cause of all four of these changes is growth in the size and complexity of business firms, together with the resultant burden on the chief executive. These trends are:

1. Greater divisionalization (change from functional to product organization) accompanied by decentralization.

2. Elaboration and changing role of corporate staff.

    a. A greater variety of staff units—e.g., addition of community relations, government relations, operations research, executive development, organization planning, long–range planning and electronic data processing units.

    b. A changing role of staff units from primarily service to more emphasis on assisting the chief executive in planning and control.

3. Emergence of group executives, i.e., a new layer of supervision between the president and the product divisions.

4. Elaboration of the chief executive's office taking such forms as:

    a. More persons in the line of command (e.g., chairman, president, executive vice president);

    b. More staff assistants of various kinds, especially in areas such as trouble shooting and special studies; or

    c. Councils or committees of top executives.

Before leaving the subject of size, I would like to note my disagreement with the common conception that size inevitably leads to impersonality, coldness, authoritarianism, conformity, and a lack of freedom and creativity.

For one thing, a small enterprise (five or ten people) with an authoritarian head leaves little room for freedom of subordinates, or for significant decision–making by them. And by virtue of knowing nearly all the details of the enterprise, the top man in such a small unit will almost invariably make all the important decisions. A large enterprise (say 25,000 employees) with an authoritarian head will almost surely have some units whose supervisors are democratically inclined, and whose subordinates, consequently, are at least relatively free to make suggestions and express new ideas. And almost certainly there will be opportunity for more leaders to develop and for more persons to exercise significant decision–making in the larger of these two enterprises. The decisions of the third or fourth echelon man in the Department of Defense are far more important than those of the first echelon man in a small retail store.

Secondly, once an organization passes a certain size (say, for example, 500 or 1,000 people), it seems to me that it becomes much more like a very large organization than a small one. The chief executive no longer can know all the employees personally, and the loyalties, personal contacts, degree of informality and patterns of behavior are controlled more by a particular segment of the enterprise than by the total enterprise.

Furthermore, small enterprises (other than those whose main purpose is to do research) rarely have the time or resources for extensive research effort. Large organizations frequently can afford such programs—thus making room for at least a certain amount of "free–wheeling". Over and above research activities, large enterprises would seem to offer more variety of work, more interesting jobs, more complex activities, more challenging assignments, and grander opportunities—all of which attract the creative, restless, risk–taking, ambitious, non–conforming individual and tend to repel the conforming, security–conscious, order–loving person.

As a practical matter, is the professor in a large university any less creative than one in a small college? Is the research engineer at General Electric or AT & T any less creative than engineers working for smaller companies? Is the management analyst or budget examiner any less free or less creative in the U.S. Bureau of the Budget than in the budget office of a small city? Does the bus driver of a large bus belonging to a large company have less important or less frequent decisions to make than the bus driver of a small bus belonging to a small bus line? Is the company commander's job in an army of 100,000 men significantly different than the company commander's job in an army of 1,000,000 men? The evidence is certainly not conclusive on the side of the small enterprise.[106]

GOVERNMENT–BUSINESS RELATIONSHIPS

Related to the increasing size of government and business is the changing nature in the relationships between them; a change which has important organizational implications for both.

One major aspect of this change is the dramatic growth in government work by contract. Many "private" companies are now engaged entirely or principally in government work. In some cases, entirely new private enterprises, such as RAND Corporation and the Institute for Defense Analysis, have been created to perform government work. Some private companies actually spend more federal tax dollars (through the contract device) than do some of our federal departments and agencies. Government is by far the biggest single customer of business. Even a single government contract can be crucial to particular companies. Witness the furor over the award of a contract for a new plane (the TFX supersonic jet fighter) to General Dynamics rather than the Boeing Aircraft Company. Moreover, the use of cost–plus contracts by government has changed the nature of business for many concerns by eliminating the risks of the marketplace. They can't lose, and they are using government capital to boot. Government-by-contract is already being referred to as the "New" New Federalism (the "Old" New Federalism meaning the situation brought about by the grant-in-aid process).[107]

This development introduces two crucial organization problems which, in my opinion, deserve much more intensive study. One is to determine under what conditions work can be done better by contract with outside enterprises and under what conditions the same work can be done better directly by government itself. The second problem is how government agencies should organize to control contract work more effectively without losing the advantages attributed to private initiative. The future will undoubtedly see some novel attempts to solve these organizational problems.

Another aspect of the changing relationships between business and government results more directly from the increased size of both—the increased role of government in our economic and social life, and the increased size of individual businesses making it imperative for government to regulate them in the public interest. Any major industrial firm today has regular and continuing contacts with and interest in such federal agencies as the Justice Department, Federal Trade Commission, National Labor Relations Board, Securities and Exchange Commission, Tariff Commission, State Department, Defense Department, Commerce Department, Labor Department, Treasury Department and others, probably including the White House. Add to this state and local executive agencies plus legislative and judicial bodies at all levels of government and you have a sizeable relationship problem. Political and administrative decisions have become as important to business success as the play of the market. In the words of Thomas R. Reid, Civic and Governmental Affairs Manager of Ford Motor Company: "What happens in business today is determined more and more by what happened in government yesterday. Government has an impact on business policy and planning at least as great as the impact of competition in the market place because government, to a large degree, determines the nature of the market place".[108]

An important organizational development in industry, just beginning to emerge in recognition of this changing pattern, is the establishment of separate governmental relations divisions or departments. Examples are the Civic and Governmental Affairs Office of the Ford Motor Company established in 1950, the Government Relations Service of the General Electric Company established in 1958, and the Public Affairs and Employee Information Section that the Western Electric Company established in 1960. Such units not only handle problems of relationships with government, but also frequently run programs aimed at encouraging intelligent and active participation by business employees in civic, political, and governmental activities. Mr. Reid has predicted that business management in the future will make the same provision in its organization structure for handling civic and governmental affairs as it undertook in the past for dealing with public relations and personnel matters.[109]

One other development which will pose complex problems of organization for the future is the creation of mixed government–business enterprises such as the Communications Satellite Corporation created by Congress in the Communications Satellite Act of 1962 to develop and operate a global commercial communications satellite system using Telstar and similar satellites. The board of directors of this new corporation consists of representatives of the government, the general public, and the communications industry. The organization problems involved in joint ownership and joint management can be seen only dimly at this point. Flexibility, imagination, and lots of experimentation will be required to solve them.[110]

Composition of the Work Force

Dramatic changes in the composition of the work force may well bring about organization adjustments.

By 1960, white collar workers had superseded blue collar as the dominant worker group in the country. This trend is illustrated by the following figures:[111]

Type of Occupation	Per Cent of Work Force	
	1920	1960
White Collar	25	43
Blue Collar	40	36
Service	8	13
Farm	27	8

Similarly, in the ten–year period 1947–1957, there was an increase of 55.0 per cent in non-production workers, as contrasted to only a one per cent increase in production workers.[112] The same trend is evident within manufacturing, where between 1950 and 1960, white collar workers increased by 46.0 per cent, manual workers by 11.5 per cent, and service workers by 4.0 per cent.[113]

This change in the direction of a greater proportion of white collar workers will undoubtedly continue since the long–term employment trend in the goods–producing industries (manufacturing, mining, construction and agriculture) which hire large proportions of blue collar workers is down, whereas the long–term employment trend in the service–producing industries (wholesale and retail trade, finance, government) which employ large proportions of white collar workers is up.

In the next decade, professional and technical workers are expected to increase at a much faster rate than skilled, semi-skilled, and unskilled workers, as follows:[114]

Occupational Group	Expected Percentage Increase Between 1960 and 1970
Professional and Technical	40
Skilled Workers	22
Semi–skilled Workers	18
Unskilled Workers	No Change

Between 1940 and 1960, professional and technical workers increased from 6.8 per cent of the labor force to 11.2 per cent— a greater percentage increase than any other category.[115] It is also noteworthy that a much larger percentage of the professional and technical personnel are working in government and industry, with a smaller proportion being self–employed.

As might be expected, the education of those making up the work force has been increasing. Thus, those entering the work force with some college education increased from five million in the 1950's to seven million in the 1960's; those who completed high school increased from seven million to nearly twelve million in the same period.[116] As automation reduces the need for manual and clerical labor, the proportion of the work force requiring better education and more brain power can be expected to continue to increase.

Better educated employees, more of whom occupy professional, technical, and white collar jobs, can be expected to be less satisfied with routine, monotonous, and non–creative jobs with little responsibility and much supervision, and to place greater emphasis on democratic, as contrasted to authoritarian, values. The pendulum may have to swing toward "freedom" and away from "authority".

In organization terms, it would seem that the changing work force will tend to bring about further decentralization, increased participation in decision–making, and new and different patterns to facilitate motivating a new kind of worker. While organization structure patterned after the military and church models worked fairly well in a manufacturing setting, new patterns may well be needed for service industries, white collar enterprises (e.g., government agencies, insurance companies, banks, research organizations), and organization units made up of highly educated employees. "Knowledge workers", as highly educated professional and technical workers have been termed, tend to want to retain their individuality. Thus, there will have to be less emphasis on consistency of treatment and seniority—prized by manual and clerical workers—and more emphasis on the differences among individuals rather than the likenesses. Yet, as more and more knowledge workers are employed in large enterprises, new ways will have to be found to enable them to work together as a team, without sacrificing their desire for individual accomplishment.

A special case of the increasing number of professional and technical workers is the rapid expansion in the number of scientists and research engineers. Since World War II a great number of companies and agencies principally engaged in research have been created, and within existing companies and agencies, research and development units have multiplied in number and strength. Moreover, persons trained in the sciences are also becoming directly involved in management problems through such areas as electronic data processing and operations research. In government, scientists have been referred to as the "new priesthood", replacing the managers who had, in turn, replaced the lawyers.

I see three principal implications for organization resulting from this sharp increase in the number of scientists in government and industry in general, and in research and development in particular.

In the first place, organization for scientific research activity will undoubtedly continue to shift away from classical organization patterns. There will be fewer (or at least, different) controls, fewer layers of supervision, less rigid organization units, with greater use of project teams which change membership as different projects are completed or initiated, more freedom to undertake self–initiated work, and higher status for research units in the overall structure.[117]

The problem of controls has been especially bothersome. The term "colleague control" as contrasted to "hierarchy control" is becoming popular as a description of the new type of control needed for work done by scientists or others who work primarily with their minds. A revealing commentary on the attitude of researchers toward control is found in the statement of one research scientist to an administrator in a well–known "think" outfit. He said, "It's all right to ask me how I'm doing on my project at coffee or lunch. But don't come to my office or telephone me to ask; and under no circumstances ask me to submit written reports on progress".

In the second place, ways will have to be found to improve relationships between the scientist and the administrator. The general problem of achieving understanding between scientists and the layman, as well as the particular problem of relationships between the scientist and the administrator, have only recently received attention in the literature.[118]

By and large the scientist and the administrator see each other as stereotypes. The scientist sees the manager as a bureaucrat, paper–shuffler, and parasite; a non–creative and unoriginal hack who serves only as an obstacle in the way of creative people trying to do a job; and a person more interested in dollars and in power than in knowledge and innovation. The manager sees the scientist as a temperamental individualist with no skills in interpersonal relations; a narrow specialist with no interest in efficiency and economy or in the overall objectives of the enterprise; a person who looks for the right answer even in fields of human affairs where there is no single solution, who purposely makes his work mysterious and objects to all types of control, and who is more interested in impressing other members of his profession than in the success of the enterprise for which he works.

Stereotypes aside, it is probably accurate to say that the scientist, or other professional, puts great emphasis on standards of quality and method in his work. The manager, on the other hand, must take into account such additional dimensions as money, time, service, and public relations. And these factors, of course, may well necessitate a compromise with professional standards. Moreover, the scientist or other professional resists making decisions until he has adequate facts to back them up. The very nature of the work of the manager requires him frequently to make decisions on the basis of evidence which the professional or scientist would regard as inadequate and insufficient.

Some new ways of organizing in the future will have to be found that will give the scientist the freedom he needs and enable the manager to facilitate rather than inhibit his work; that will give the manager the control he needs to insure that the work of the scientists is contributing to the achievement of the objectives of the enterprise and remains in proper balance with other activities; and that will enable both parties to communicate effectively with each other based on mutual respect for the contributions of both. If the gap between the scientist and non–scientist continues to increase, a wholly new organization unit might have to be created for the sole purpose of trying to bridge it.

In the third place, while the great need for scientists who are truly creative and innovative is now well recognized in both industry and government, there are clearly a limited number of people with the intellectual capacity and creative nature to fill the need. As a result, new ways to organize must be found that will utilize these limited resources to the maximum extent.

There are other changes in the composition of the work force that will have an effect on the organization of the future. For example, a greater proportion of the work force will be made up of women. It has been estimated that by 1970, 55 per cent of women between the ages of forty–five and fifty–five will be trying to earn a living.[119] No mere man would have the temerity to predict what the result on organization will be.

Another change in the work force over the next decade or two is that there will be a greater proportion of young and old workers. The number of workers in the thirty to forty–five age bracket will be the same or less.[120] These, by and large, are the people now holding down middle management jobs. If it is true that there will be less need for middle managers in the future as some predict,[121] this change in the proportion of workers may alleviate the strain resulting from the elimination of middle management jobs.

RATE OF TECHNOLOGICAL CHANGE

Bruce D. Henderson, Vice President of Arthur D. Little, Inc., has said, "The most significant fact of our times, overshadow-

ing all else, is the tremendous *rate* of change that we are ex-
periencing".[122] In the same vein, a report of The Foundation
for Research on Human Behavior states: "Small businesses,
large industrial organizations, and whole governments find
they must devote an increasing proportion of their organizational resources to introducing, engineering, and handling
change".[123]

If one were to plot against time, scientific and technological
developments of almost any kind, he would get a chart that
would look something like that shown in Figure 14.

The general consequence of this factor is that agencies and
companies must be organized to cope with change, to expect it
as the ordinary course of affairs and not as a traumatic experience. The importance of organizing the government to cope
with such change has been well stated by James L. McCamy as
follows:

Acceleration in science and technology is so much faster than
reorganization to match it that the nation is in more peril from
chaotic administration than from any other nation's superior

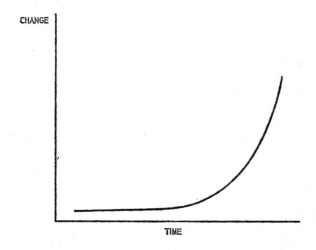

FIGURE 14. SCIENTIFIC AND TECHNOLOGICAL CHANGE

technology. If we become a second-rate power, we will fail not in science but in the administration of science.[124]

In more specific terms, I foresee some seven developments relating to organization growing out of awareness of the impact of rapid change.

In the first place, top management will have to recognize its responsibility for setting a climate that will anticipate, accept, and welcome organizational changes as needed to meet technological and other environmental changes.[125] The emphasis will have to be on flexibility, informality, and more frequent intuitive decisions rather than on stability, formal structure, and reliance on old orthodoxies.

Secondly, and contrary to most present doctrine, there will have to be less rigid and less spelled–out views on the objectives of an enterprise, since specifying them in detail inhibits prompt change in objectives to meet change in environment and technology. Along this line, Sherman Kingsbury of Arthur D. Little, Inc., has stated:

> One would like to start describing Arthur D. Little by saying what it is for, what are its objectives, but even this leads immediately into difficulty. There is no single set of objectives for the organization that all significant members would agree upon as an adequate statement. Certainly, there has never existed a formal statement from the management as to what corporate objectives are. There have been attempts to explain the organization and its evolved objectives; there have been attempts to influence these; there have not been attempts by management to legislate arbitrary change or codification of these: few members of the organization think this would be appropriate, and most would resist it actively and probably successfully were management to attempt it.[126]

As one of my friends has put it, "a little bit of chaos now is desirable if it prevents a lot of chaos later".

Thirdly, there will be less rigid job descriptions and less rigid definitions of responsibility. The new concept of a job description will be that it should not describe a job as it is now, but rather be so worded as to permit the person in the job to undertake anything new that comes up which he is capable of handling. Similarly, there will be much less emphasis on detailed experience for a particular job, and more on the individual's flexibility, adaptability, inventiveness, and ability to grow. A striking example of the advantage of "little" as compared to "much" experience can be found in the following quotation:

> In the years from 1861–1871 ten steel companies in the country (U.S.) began making steel by the new Bessemer process. All but one of them at the outset imported from Great Britain English workmen familiar with the process. One, the Cambria Company, did not. In the first few years those companies with British labor established an initial superiority. But by the end of the 70's Cambria had obtained a commanding lead over all competitors.
>
> The Bessemer process, like any new technique, had been constantly improved and refined in this period from 1861–1871. The British laborers of Cambria's competitors, secure in the performance of their own original techniques, resisted and resented all change. The Pennsylvania farm boys, untrammeled by the rituals and traditions of their craft, happily and rapidly adapted themselves to the constantly changing process. They ended by creating an unassailable competitive position for their company.[127]

A fourth consequence of the "revolution in rate of change" may well be the need to adjust the widely accepted "equilibrium" model of organization. This model holds that organizations are in equilibrium, that forces for change are introduced, that the organization adjusts to these forces, after which the organization reaches a new equilibrium. It strikes me that this model puts too much emphasis on equilibrium, in the sense of the organization seeking stability and security, and on change as an episodic phenomenon. Moreover, this model assumes that equilibrium is an end, rather than merely a means toward achieving such objectives as growth, progress and productivity. It may well be that under certain circumstances, equilibrium should purposely be upset to achieve such ends.

What we need is a new model or concept which regards change as a continuing process, which recognizes that change may mean ambiguity and uncertainty but that these results are not necessarily "bad", and which sees the organization as constantly changing (whether rapidly or slowly) rather than reaching set stages of equilibrium in between periods of change.[128] To a certain extent, the approach described in my next point moves in this direction.

A significant attempt to meet the problem of rapid change, adopted more and more frequently in recent years, is to organize by task force, rather than by fixed organization units.[129] This approach involves using a team drawn from various parts of the enterprise for a specific task or project. When that task or project is completed, the members of the team return to their original organization units or are assigned to new project teams. Thus, each team has a temporary life span and cuts across traditional organization lines. Such a plan was recently adopted in the engineering design work of the Port Authority. Prior to the change, engineering design work was performed by fixed organization units in the mechanical, electrical, structural and architectural fields. Under the new plan, these units were abolished, and project teams made up of an appropriate number of each type of specialist were set up to handle active projects in process. Small staff units of senior men in each specialty were set up to advise and assist the project teams.

The task force approach permits substantial flexibility since members with appropriate skills can be added or subtracted from the team as needed, new teams can be set up rapidly to handle new projects, and team members tend to be "purpose" or "objective" oriented rather than "process" oriented. The major problem is to schedule staff so as to keep them in full use.

The way this organizational setup works out in Arthur D. Little, Inc., has been described as follows:

Thus, there are two significant organizations operating simultaneously in ADL. The first (and generally agreed to be the most important) is the organization of the work going on at any particular time. The second, which operates to support the first, is the administrative organization.

The significant unit of work organization is the case. This is an assignment from a particular client to carry out a specified task in an agreed period of time for a specified amount of money. ... The team ... is chosen ... on the basis of the nature of the work and the commitments of the people who are considered for membership. The average life time of such a case unit is on the order of six months. When the assignment is ended, the team collapses and the members become involved in other activities to take up the time released. On the average, a staff member is active in two to four or more cases at any given time, depending on the nature of his training and his experience in the company. ...

The work organization is in charge of getting the work done and operates with a time perspective appropriate to the demands of the work. The administrative organization operates with the longer time perspective appropriate to maintaining and adapting a setting within which the work organization can function and the staff can find fulfillment.[130]

A somewhat similar approach to the use of task forces is referred to as program management and is commonly used in defense industries.[131] Here a program manager, or project manager, with perhaps a small number of accountants or control officers, is designated to "manage" or "coordinate" a particular complex contract requiring work by a number of different divisions. The bulk of the employees doing the work, however, remain in their regular organizational units and continue to report to their regular supervisors. The object of this approach is to achieve flexibility without undue disruption from shifting people out of their normal working relationships too often and too sharply. The program or project manager is ordinarily accountable for results but does not have authority to issue orders to the various operating units. How, then, does he achieve his objective? Primarily through informal means and such techniques as persuasion, leadership, cooperation, consultation and compromise.

Another consequence of rapid change is the recognition that more emphasis needs to be given to long range planning[132] and to the continuing study of the external environment and the effect changes in that environment will have on the policies, management and organization of the enterprise. A good example is General Electric's environmental factors studies which included a series of reports entitled "1980: The Basic Planning Horizon", which were aimed at presenting a picture of the business environment twenty years into the future. Illustrative titles of these reports were "The Economy in 1980", "International Economic Relations", "Raw Materials and Energy", "Housing and Family Living", and "A Social Science View of Forces Shaping Future Markets". This kind of approach made it possible, for example, for the company to predict at an early date the use of teaching machines in the schools.[133]

A similar example can be found in the recently published book entitled "Metropolitan Transportation—1980", prepared by the Comprehensive Planning Office of The Port of New York Authority. This work identifies basic trends in the New York– New Jersey metropolitan region as a basis for formulating future specific transportation programs. It attempts to identify the factors which have brought about trends currently evident, as well as those which may be expected to bring about changes in the future.

Lastly, to meet the challenge of change, it would seem desirable in many cases to establish a special organization unit whose job is to question everything, including the objectives of the enterprise. Such a concept has been proposed by one of the leading insurance company executives in the country who recommends that there be a "vice president for revolution".[134]

Very probably, to manage today's enterprise effectively, in the face of rapid technological and social change, we need more managers who would fit George Bernard Shaw's statement that

"The reasonable man adapts himself to the world; the unreasonable one persists in trying to adapt the world to himself. Therefore all progress depends on the unreasonable man".

AUTOMATION, ELECTRONIC DATA PROCESSING AND THE COMPUTER

Until recent years, the word "automation" has meant to most people the substitution of machines for human beings in the performance of manual labor. As of now, the concept of automation has been broadened substantially to include also the substitution of machines for man in the processing of mass data at great speed, in the making of certain kinds of decisions, and in the exercise of control, or "feedback", to adjust automatically certain processes or operations. The development of the electronic computer has helped make these new functions feasible.

Since the installation of the first computer for business–type data processing in 1950, there has been an explosive growth in the use of computers and electronic data processing in both industry and government. By the end of 1964, there were approximately 17,500 digital, or data–processing, computer installations in the country.[135] The number of electronic computers in the federal government, exclusive of those used for tactical and classified purposes in the Department of Defense, increased from 90 as of June 30, 1956 to 1,326 as of June 30, 1963, and was expected to increase to 2,150 by June 30, 1966.[136] As a matter of fact, computers have become so pervasive in government that they are referred to as the new version of "machine politics".

Probably the best–known prediction of the impact of automation and related developments on organization is that made by Harold J. Leavitt and Thomas L. Whisler in their provocative article "Management in the 1980's".[137] These authors argue that since the computer will make many decisions currently made by middle managers, many fewer such managers will be needed in the future and their role will be less important.[138] The organization of the future, according to Leavitt and Whisler, will look not like a pyramid, but rather like a football on top of a bell, with a fairly distinct line of demarcation between them.

The football represents top management which will be concerned with creative, unprogrammed, complex, highly important, and one-of-a-kind decisions. Top management will contain many highly specialized staff assistants, do more of the planning than previously, and will make more group decisions. Leavitt and Whisler feel that it is also possible that eventually the computer will make some of these types of decisions. They don't go quite so far as Herbert A. Simon, however, who states that "technologically, machines will be capable, within twenty years, of doing any work that a man can do", although he notes that there may be economic or other advantages to having man continue to do certain kinds of work.[139]

The bell represents the rest of the organization. It is similar to the present pyramid, and contains the people who will be carrying out programmed or routine activities.[140] In a similar analysis, Dr. Simon Ramo has invented the word "intellectronics" to describe the man–machine system in which machines perform the routine, high quantity intellectual tasks, while man tackles the creative, imaginative, subtle and complex tasks.[141]

The principal point of controversy over the effect on organization of automation and the computer is the question of whether the result will be further centralization or further decentralization. Here it is necessary to distinguish between two types of centralization–decentralization. One has to do with the actual processing of data (i.e., the way information is gathered, arranged and stored). For this type, there is general agreement that the trend will be toward centralization. The second has to do with decision–making (i.e., the way the information is used). For this type, there is no agreement, even among sophisticated observers.

Leavitt and Whisler, as we have seen, believe that decision–making will be centralized. Herbert A. Simon, unlike Leavitt and Whisler, believes that the automation of data processing will not change in any major way the fundamental hierarchical (pyramidal) structure. Nevertheless, he still concludes that these new developments "will tend to induce more centralization in decision–making activities at middle management levels".[142]

On the other side, John F. Burlingame argues: "Indeed, if we couple our experience in decentralized organizations with a realistic evaluation of the nature and extent of the future impact of information technology in such organizations, we can establish a very reasonable basis for concluding that decentralization and the middle manager are much more likely to *grow* and *flourish* than to wither and die in the decades ahead".[143] Similarly, Joseph A. Raffaele states: "In short, the impact of technology on management points to a diffusion of leadership and self–government".[144]

Two principal arguments are made by those who foresee centralization of decision–making. One is that since more information will be made available more rapidly to top management, especially information pertaining to *inter–relationships* between functions, top management will be able to make decisions formerly made by separate departments or divisions. Thus, decisions formerly made by marketing or production segments of the organization because information was not available on how to tie them together, can now better be made by top management with knowledge of the impact of each on the other. Or to take another example, decisions formerly made by units concerned only with highways, airports, or rails, can now be made at a higher level based on information about how decisions on one type of transportation affect all other types.

The second argument is that decisions formerly made at lower levels because of the necessity for fast action, can now be made centrally with no loss of time because of the immediate availability of necessary information. Thus, the State Department could theoretically act just about as fast as an ambassador in the field plus having available more of some kinds of information on which to base the decision.

The arguments of those on the other side (i.e., those predicting decentralization), paradoxically, start with the same premise: more and faster information. These people argue, however, that since more and better information will be available to lower levels, decisions can be made there with *less* risk of being wrong than previously. Further, more, better and faster information to top management makes for more effective control, alerting top management sooner as to when things are getting out of control and enabling them to hold subordinates accountable for results more rationally and more specifically. And in addition, with more and better information available to top management, such officials will be able to spend time realistically on long range problems, innovation, and meeting environmental changes, delegating other types of decisions formerly made by them to the lower levels.

The practicing executive tends to support the view that automation and the computer either will mean greater decentralization or at least won't stop the overall trend toward decentralization. Based on a survey of top executives in large United States industrial corporations, for example, Otis Lipstreu concludes: "... The supervisor will surely regain some of his lost discretionary authority. Automaticity of work requires that he make decisions at the work level quickly, decisions which formerly were made at higher levels in the hierarchy. His work will increasingly resemble that of present middle management . . . ." [145]

Similarly, a study of over 200 major corporations made by *American Business* found that less than one in ten executives thought that electronic data processing would reverse the trend toward decentralized management.[146] This same view is supported in a survey made by the Organization Division, Civil Service Commission, Canada, which found that in companies with five to ten years of experience with computers, there was little or no effect on organization structure.[147]

As for my own views as to the probable effect on organization of automation and the computer, they can be summed up, as you might suppose, by the phrase "it all depends". It's difficult for me to imagine the same effect on the organization of a manufacturing company, a law firm, a United States embassy abroad, and a personnel office. Not only will the results undoubtedly vary with the type of enterprise or kind of work involved, but also with the philosophy, values and assumptions of particular top executives. I can think of a number of charismatic executives, for example, who would never permit the substitution of the judgment of a machine for their own "infallible" judgment.

But by and large, I do not believe that the impact on organization of automation and the computer will be as great as many predict.[148] Possibly this is because of the natural reaction of a human being to resist the idea that he may be replaced by a machine—especially by a "thinking" machine. But perhaps this same subconscious fear has led some to overemphasize the possible results. This reaction is illustrated by two of my favorite cartoons. One shows an operator asking a computer, "Is there a God?", and the computer replying, "There is now". The other shows the operator reading the tape coming out of a computer and saying, "It says, 'Cogito ergo sum' ".

Basically, the computer provides more information than may have been previously available, and provides it faster. But so did conventional punched card (tabulating) equipment when it was introduced. And the use of this latter type equipment had no fundamental effect on organization or decision-making. Moreover, executives have long had more information than they can handle. The problem is not how to add to this flow of information so much as it is how to decide what information is important, how to digest it, and what to do about it. Information not worth having is not worth having faster and more accurately.

The Port of New York Authority has been using a computer on a large variety of projects since early in the 1950's. There has been no discernible impact of such use on either the formal or the informal organization.

The complexity, ambiguities, and intangibles of organization, together with the fact that organizational decisions are directly affected by power, politics, status, and value judgments, lead me to believe that automation, the computer, and electronic data processing can constitute only one element going into decisions on organization—and a relatively small one at that.

It has been predicted that a computer will become the chess champion of the world.[149] This is certainly possible. The computer is already making many technical decisions for management. But as John F. Burlingame has pointed out with regard to chess, it presents "a problem which has no unknowns—even where the rules of play are completely defined, where the scope of action is limited, where the relationships between the elements are explicit, where there is but a single, defined objective, where the value system is determined and unambiguous, and where the problem is precisely the same now as it was 100 years ago and as it will be 100 years from now".[150]

Thus, while the computer may soon outmatch the Petrosians, the Botvinniks and the Fischers, I believe that it will be a long, long time, if ever, before a computer will be able to decide for a manager such a relatively simple problem in his day's work as what to say to a subordinate who comes to work late.[151]

It may well be that computers can, or will be able to duplicate man's rational and analytical processes.[152] But many decisions are also, appropriately, influenced by emotions, feelings, and moral values—such as love, hate, fear, loyalty, hope, and compassion.[153] Imagine, if you can, a computer trying to decide whether a man should give up his place in a lifeboat to a woman or child. Undoubtedly, the computer will be able to *answer* more and more questions. But will it be able to *ask* the right questions? Rather than replacing the executive, the computer is apt to enhance his job by identifying new problems, revealing new complexities, and providing new opportunities.

If tolerance for ambiguity, skill in diagnosing and solving interpersonal relations problems, willingness to take risks (i.e., "stick your neck out"), and ability to motivate and inspire others—not to mention courage, character, and zest—are important attributes of an effective manager, and I believe that they are, I can't help wondering how the computer would score on these measures.

One additional word on the effect of the computer and electronic data processing. The computer requires a big investment. I worry that once bought (or rented), and once programmed, it may actually inhibit change. There may be a tendency not to want to change, or perhaps even not to discover that there are still better ways. We may have discovered in the computer a technique for insuring the continuation of the "one best way" fallacy of the early scientific management thinkers. The ultimate result might well be, as someone once said, "instant inefficiency.[154] Or as one perceptive observer has put it: "The greatest danger in modern technology isn't that machines will begin to think like men, but that men will begin to think like machines".[155]

The computer might well make "safe" (i.e., mediocre) decisions. Would it make great ones? For example, a computer might have advised against the American revolution as having too little chance of success!

OPERATIONS RESEARCH AND MANAGEMENT GAMES

There is no common agreement on a definition of "Operations Research"—even among those who regard themselves as specialists in this field. For my purposes, I will define it as the application of sophisticated mathematical and scientific tools and the technique of simulation (model–building) to the problems of management. Since management games constitute one way of simulating the problems of management, I will discuss this technique along with operations research.

A whole new literature and profession have developed in this area since World War II. And the operations research approach has produced dramatic results on certain types of operating, production, and procedural problems. Most operations research projects to date, however, have been based on a cost–benefit analysis. This approach makes the assumption that economics is the principal factor to be considered and leaves out (or severely de–emphasizes) human beings and all their other motivations. Perhaps it is for this reason that operations research has rarely, if ever, been used to solve an overall agency or company organization problem.

There is no doubt that many operations research projects have resulted in some organizational changes in the way work is handled in small units, or for particular functions such as warehousing or inventory control (i.e., in both cases for a "sub–system"). But these projects were not designed to improve organization per se. There are a few current experiments in which the operations research approach is actually being used to test how different organization patterns will work. For example, RAND Corporation, on behalf of the Air Force, has been using "game simulation" to test different patterns of organization, using a computer to speed up the process.[156] While apparently providing valuable information, this type of simulation should not be confused with reality. The mere fact that time has been shortened, plus the fact that the consequences of mistakes are different, changes the nature of the problem to some degree.

Similarly, a number of universities, notably the University of Illinois[157] and Carnegie Institute of Technology,[158] have been using management games as a teaching device in the field of organization. Part of the process has involved comparing results under different organization patterns with other variables held constant. The conclusions developed are interesting, and in some cases raise provocative questions about some currently accepted organization "dogma". Nevertheless, there is considerable difference between college students working for grades, or if not working for grades, "playing a game", and a going government agency or private business whose employees are mature adults working at making a living and getting ahead in a "culture" considerably different than that of a university. Thus, while this approach may well be an effective teaching device in terms of arousing interest and giving the student some flavor of how groups work together, its value in providing lessons on how to organize a particular going concern is limited.

The Organization Planning Unit of the United States Rubber Company has also been doing some laboratory experimentation simulating different organization patterns in the hope of being able to predict, with greater assurance, the effect of changing a given organization in any specific way. The officials involved believe that the success of laboratory methods in dealing with problems of group dynamics may have some carry-over with respect to problems of organization.[159]

My own view is that while it might be possible to simulate varying formal patterns of organization with some relationship to reality, it would be extremely difficult to do so for the informal organization. Moreover, the tyranny of mathematical formulae and mathematical models is that they force the "real" world, which consists of quantitative, qualitative, and unknown factors, into an artificial world where everything relevant and important has to be assigned a number.[160] As C. Mansel Keene has said, "There are . . . those who feel uncomfortable without final answers so they concern themselves mentally and emotionally in the tangible and dismiss any broader area of relevance as destroying the integrity of their field of endeavor".[161] The most important problem in decision-making is not quantification of data. The real problems are determining what factors are relevant, how relevant they are, and what basic values and assumptions are held by the decision-maker.

My own preference is for experimentation on the job in the actual setting. To a certain extent, managers do such "trial and error" experimenting all the time. But it could be done more consciously and with better scientific controls. This approach is especially feasible under certain circumstances, as when a new unit is being created, a key executive is retiring, or a new chief executive has taken over. An excellent example of this type of organizational experimentation can be found in Project Focus of the U. S. Federal Aviation Agency.[162]

The principal arguments against this approach, as compared with the simulation or laboratory approach, are the possible prohibitive cost of making a mistake, the length of time it takes to test varying patterns, and the difficulty of controlling all the variables that may be present. In my judgment, the reality of this approach (if properly controlled) usually justifies the time and possible risk. There are undoubtedly some cases where the risk of failure would be so great that one would decide not to experiment. I believe that such cases are rare. Too frequently what we fail to realize is the hidden cost of doing something inefficiently simply because, never having tried any other approach, we are unaware that one exists.

RESEARCH FINDINGS

Undoubtedly, the findings of present and future research, whether directly in the field of organization or in related fields of the behavioral and social sciences, will affect the how and why of organizing in the years to come. However, if the past is any guide, these research findings may have relatively little impact on practitioners for reasons I shall try to analyze below.

In the field of organization alone, there has been considerable research in recent years. This research has followed many different paths, partly, as Mason Haire has pointed out, because of different views as to what the problem is.[163] Professor Haire has identified five major approaches, based largely on five recurring issues: [164]

1. The conflict between personality and organization—i.e., the individual's needs *vs*. the demands of the enterprise.

2. Organization structure—i.e., linkages, levels and bonds, with a central concern for communications.

3. Decision theory.

4. Ecology of organizations—i.e., the economic, legal, social, and technological environment and its effect on organization.

5. Forces tending toward the survival or destruction of organizations.

In most or all of these approaches, there has been a tendency by recent scholars to use model–building and sophisticated mathematical techniques as prime analytical tools.

Books could be (and have been) written on the research being carried out in each of these areas. I have found the works of Herbert A. Simon,[165] who focuses on decision–making, to be particularly sound as a framework for thinking about the problem of organizing, and the works of Chris Argyris,[166] who focuses on the problem of the individual *vs.* the organization, particularly provocative.

Argyris' thesis is that the traditional hierarchical, or pyramidal, organization structure rewards the immature, dependent, and submissive person and penalizes the mature, independent, and creative person. The result is absenteeism, turnover, apathy, and self–imposed or group–imposed limitations on production. He sees the commonly proposed remedies of human relations, job enlargement, and democratic leadership as weak or useless cures. Instead, he advocates "reality–oriented leadership" (i.e., a variety of leadership patterns to fit specific situations); a flat organization structure in which pay is related to one's contribution to a particular process rather than his level in the hierarchy, and in which the group rather than "management" sets the rules; and a change from emphasis on management or supervisory controls to self–controls. He also sees the possibility in the future of several different patterns of organization structure existing simultaneously in the same enterprise, each being used to solve different types of problems.

Despite the fact that there has been considerable research on organization and related fields in recent years, and that much of it is exciting and potentially rewarding, its usefulness to (or use by) practitioners has been limited. I have asked numerous top organization planners in government and industry to tell me specifically how they have used any of these research results in their work. Many of them have simply said "not at all"; others have replied in such vague or indirect terms as to leave me with no tangible examples.

In part, of course, this state of affairs can be blamed on the practitioner—on his lack of knowledge about research findings, on his suspicions about the value of what the "academic" researchers produce, on his natural reactions to what John M. Pfiffner has called the "anti–management" bias of the social scientists,[167] or simply on his being so busy putting out fires and trying to get acceptance of the most simple and mundane elements of good management that he hasn't had time to absorb new knowledge and sophisticated refinements.[168]

But in large part, I believe, the fault lies in the form and content of the research findings made available. For one thing, much that has passed for research has in reality been nothing more than armchair theorizing about organization. Such research usually produces sweeping generalizations unsupported by facts or without rigorous attention to the circumstances which may make the propositions put forward true or not true, and the degree to which they are true or not true. Moreover, the propositions are frequently made in new language, so that if the practitioner does take the trouble to puzzle them out, he discovers nothing more than "old wine in new bottles". Much of this type of theorizing is done by candidates for the doctoral degree who feel the need to make a contribution, and do it either by cutting the pie in a new way, or by attacking accepted doctrine.

The researchers have given cause for suspicion of their work by not rigorously analyzing their own assumptions. Early management theorists assumed that people were much like machines, and got certain results. Many current researchers, with social science training, assume that people are, or want to be, free, responsible, creative, mature, etc. Naturally, they get different results.[169]

Bernard Berelson and Gary A. Steiner, in a recent book entitled *Human Behavior: An Inventory of Scientific Findings*,[170] find the following things wrong with present behavioral science research: "too much precision misplaced on trivial matters, too little respect for crucial facts as against grand theories, too much respect for insights that are commonplace, too much indication and too little proof, too little genuine cumulation of generalizations, too little regard for the learning of the past, far too much jargon".

George A. Shipman, in commenting on the same problem states that "the usual research strategies . . . tend to be too elaborate, too expensive, too time–consuming, and often too inconclusive to support remedial action".[171] And Mason Haire attributes the difficulty to the fact that social science research has been too general (basic) or too specific (applied); what is needed is something in between (developmental research) that will show how the ideas produced by the social sciences can be used in practice.[172]

What is needed is more empirical research in depth—involving the testing of specific hypotheses either in actual situations, or possibly through simulation. The research findings most frequently cited by practitioners as having either been used by them, or as influencing their thinking, are those dealing with the Hawthorne Plant of Western Electric,[173] the Harwood Manufacturing Company,[174] and the various enterprises studied by the Survey Research Center of the University of Michigan.[175] All of these were intensive studies of particular problems in particular companies or agencies. A number of more recent case studies, such as those by Paul R. Lawrence[176] and Robert H. Guest[177] are of a similar nature and may turn out to be similarly influential. It is studies like these, plus those being conducted under the auspices of the Inter–University Case Program and the Institute of Governmental Studies of the University of California,[178] that would seem to have the most promise.

Of course, it is not easy to produce studies like the ones I have mentioned. There are few government agencies and few private companies willing to spend the money or take the risks

involved in sponsoring research which may produce results that
are unfavorable (to them), disrupt operations, or upset a delicate balance of power among key executives. Even when research is permitted, there are few sponsoring units willing to
see the results published in un–Bowdlerized form. There are
few observers sufficiently objective to "find" results which may
disprove their pet theses. There are few situations which aren't
changed substantially by the very presence of the researchers.
And there are usually so many variables present as to make it
questionable whether the findings are applicable in any other
environment.

If and when that utopia arrives wherein social scientists can
translate their findings into English, and mathematically–
oriented researchers their findings into words, we will have
significantly narrowed the gap between the researcher and the
practitioner.[179] Accomplishing this result might necessitate dis-
covering some way of motivating researchers to want to see their
findings put into practice, rather than merely published to im-
press their learned colleagues.

Despite all the difficulties, research must and will go on. And
despite the amount of current research on problems of organizing, the surface has barely been scratched. Organization
problems urgently needing study include the relationship of
culture to organizational assumptions and principles,[180] the
relation of size to organizational assumptions and principles,
the relation of level in the hierarchy to organizational assumptions and principles, how to organize to insure innovation and
foresight as well as efficient operations, how to organize to insure democratic responsiveness as well as efficient operations,
how to organize for more effective relationships between the
manager and the technical specialist or professional, how the
formal and informal organization can best be related to each
other, the effect of different patterns of organization on motivation, the relationship between organization and communication (not only man-man communication, but also man-machine
and machine-machine), how to achieve the advantages of de-

centralization without sacrificing those of centralization, and the most effective relationship between headquarters staff units and staff units at lower levels in the enterprise.

The subjects I have just listed deal directly with various aspects of organization. An almost infinite number of subjects present themselves if one thinks in terms of studies to determine how recent findings in the social and behavioral sciences may affect organization.[181]

One final word on social science research. As has been seen, I am skeptical of the value to government and industry of research done in the laboratory or with college students. I am also skeptical of the value of research findings based on a project in one enterprise to other enterprises whose total situations are different. Nevertheless, I have no doubt that social scientists can make a real and practical contribution to a particular enterprise by research in that enterprise.[182]

OTHER SOCIAL AND TECHNOLOGICAL FACTORS

In addition to the major social and technological developments already discussed, there are, of course, many others that will in all probability have a noticeable impact on organization in the future.

One development that might prove interesting, for example, is the shorter work week. The result well might be in the direction of "dual platoons" as in football, with two (or possibly even three) organization charts. Even if the charts are identical, except for the names of the "players", the informal organization (if we accept the implications of much that I have said about the relationship of organization and people) will undoubtedly be different.

Other developments that occur to me as possibly important for those concerned with organization include the population explosion, the continued growth of cities and metropolitan areas, the increasing mobility of people in this country, cold (or hot) war developments, the common market and other international economic changes, changes in views as to ethical or "proper" behavior, the "revolution of rising expectations" in the underdeveloped countries of the world, changing views on race relations in this country,[183] and, for business if not for government, the continued change from the "owner-manager" to the "professional manager", the decline in relative power of the board of directors, and the recognition of other goals for the enterprise in addition to profit maximization.

By Way of Summary

The precise impact on organization of all the social and technological developments that I have mentioned, plus many others not now foreseeable, is cloudy, and in many respects, contradictory. It is interesting to contemplate possible cause-effect relationships. But it is probably better organization theory to put such speculation aside and to organize on the basis of the specific situation at hand, maintaining sufficient flexibility and an adequate climate for acceptance of change to enable quick reorganization when circumstances dictate.

The more we study the problem of organization, the more we recognize its complexity, its dynamics, its variety, its pluralism, its paradoxes, and its contradictions. One might even say that organization, like war, is essentially disorderly.[184] Organizational decisions are, and will be, based on probabilities, not absolutes. And generalizations about organization are notable for the number of qualifications, limitations, and exceptions to them. In recognition of these facts, we no longer search for "the one best organization"; we recognize that different types of organization may be appropriate for different types of work, different kinds of people and different environmental conditions; and we acknowledge that what is the best organization today may be much less than the best tomorrow.

How should one organize? It all depends. Depends on what?

Some of the answers, I hope, may be found above. Others may be provided by future research. But many of the answers will continue to be based on insight, intuition, intelligence, inspiration, ingenuity, and plain old trial and error.

notes

1. My description of the Sears Roebuck case is taken from the excellent account in William Foote Whyte, *Man and Organization: Three Problems in Human Relations in Industry* (Homewood, Ill.: Richard D. Irwin, 1959), pp. 12–16.

2. For a similar, but more elaborate, analysis of the two general types of managers, and the results obtained by each, see Douglas McGregor, *The Human Side of Enterprise* (New York: McGraw–Hill, 1960).

3. Organizing on a pragmatic basis means not only "doing what works" to carry out given objectives effectively. It also means "doing what works" to determine objectives. This is in line with current thinking that management is not only "getting things done through people" but also "deciding what to do"; it is not only solving problems, but also anticipating, preventing, changing, or even creating problems where necessary. While decisions as to what objectives to adopt undoubtedly depend upon value judgments that are outside the concept of pragmatism, from the point of view of organizing pragmatically to determine objectives, "doing what works" means to organize so as to bring to bear on such decisions the various interests involved and the best knowledge and skills available, insuring that the decision is made at the appropriate level, and providing an effective mechanism for evaluating the result of such decisions.

4. All those who have served in the U. S. Infantry will remember that the correct answer to nearly any problem in tactics was "It depends on the situation and the terrain".

5. See Appendix A for a selected list of definitions. For an excellent discussion of the many difficulties involved in defining the term "organization", see Herbert Kaufman, "Why Organizations Behave As They Do: An Outline of a Theory", a paper presented at An Interdisciplinary Seminar on Administrative Theory, Mar. 20–21, 1961, at the University of Texas, Austin, pp. 38 ff.

6. This is a modified version of a definition suggested by the National Industrial Conference Board. (*Corporate Organization Structures*, Studies in Personnel Policy No. 183, 1961, page 5.)

7. I shall generally use the word "enterprise" as the generic term to include both private companies and government agencies.

8. Some of my more sophisticated social science friends would probably prefer the phrase, "differentiation of roles".

9. For an excellent summary of the reasons why the distinction between management in government and in industry has been narrowing, see Austin J. Tobin, address in acceptance of the annual award of the Henry Laurence Gantt Medal, at the Hotel Roosevelt, New York City, Sept. 25, 1962. For some supporting and some contrary views, see Robert N. Anthony, "New Frontiers in Financial Management", *The Federal Accountant*, 11 (June, 1962), p. 25; William J. Siffin, "Business Administration $\neq$ Public Administration", *Business Horizons* 5 (Winter, 1962), pp. 69–76; and James F. Guyot, "Government Bureaucrats *Are* Different", *Public Administration Review*, 22 (December, 1962), pp. 195–202.

10. For support of this point see the Anthony and Guyot references in the previous footnote.

11. Letter from Kahn to Sherman, dated Apr. 21, 1959.

12. For more detail on this new relationship, see Chap. 5, pages 129–131, and especially the first reference cited in footnote 107, at pages 1103–05.

13. Austin J. Tobin, *op. cit.*

14. *Dun's Review and Modern Industry*, 76 (September, 1960), p. 40.

15. See Appendix B for the entire manual section dealing with the general subject of organization in the Port Authority. For an account of general industrial practice with respect to where responsibility for organization planning is located, see Joseph K. Bailey, "Organization Planning: Whose Responsibility?", *Academy of Management Journal*, 7 (June, 1964), pp. 95–108.

16. The problems resulting for the foreman because of the many decisions made for him by industrial engineers and other staff groups are graphically portrayed in Fritz J. Roethlisberger, "The Foreman:

Master and Victim of Double Talk", *Harvard Business Review*, 23 (Spring, 1945), pp. 283–298.

17. This analysis follows closely that of Luther Gulick in "Notes On the Theory of Organization", in Luther Gulick and L. Urwick (eds.), *Papers on the Science of Administration* (New York: Institute of Public Administration, 1937), pp. 3–45. For a critical analysis of this approach, see Herbert A. Simon, *Administrative Behavior* (New York: Macmillan, 1947), Chap. II. For an analysis closely resembling that of Gulick's, see Aristotle's *Politics*, Book IV, Chap. 15.

18. This change has generally been referred to in industry as "divisionalization", and the product divisions are frequently referred to as "profit centers". For an example of some of the benefits achieved by a specific company making such a reorganization, see Scott Nicholson, "A Problem in Organization", *Dun's Review and Modern Industry*, 81 (June, 1963), pp. 43–44, 68, 72. See also footnote 58.

19. For a more elaborate, and somewhat different, treatment of the advantages and disadvantages of the process and functional types of organization in government, see Robert T. Golembiewski, "Civil Service and Managing Work: Some Unintended Consequences", *American Political Science Review*, 56 (December, 1962), pp. 964–969.

20. In this case, the clientele served corresponds to the purposes of the organization, and therefore the organization structure would likely be as shown in Fig. 3.

21. *Public Administration Review*, 6 (Winter, 1946), pp. 53–67. The same material is covered in Professor Simon's *Administrative Behavior* (New York: Macmillan, 1947), Chap. II. The revised edition of this work (New York: Macmillan, 1957) contains the same text but adds interpretative data in a new introduction. For further discussion of Professor Simon's thesis see Edward C. Banfield's book review of the second edition, "The Decision–Making Schema," *Public Administration Review*, 17 (Autumn, 1957), pp. 278–285, and Professor Simon's reply, " 'The Decision–Making Schema': A Reply", *Public Administration Review*, 18 (Winter, 1958), pp. 60–63.

22. In its most extreme form, this principle is sometimes stated as "The span of control should not exceed from five to seven subordinates reporting to the same supervisor". The best recent discussion I have seen of the problem of span of control is Gerald G. Fisch, "Stretching the Span of Management", *Harvard Business Review*, 41 (September–October, 1963), pp. 74–85. For an interesting attempt to determine the span of control by a formula similar to those used in job evaluation see Harold Stieglitz, "Optimizing Span of Control", *Management Record*, 24 (September, 1962), pp. 25–29.

23. "Do Federal Managers Manage?", *Public Administration Review*, 22 (Spring, 1962), pp. 59–64.

24. *Ibid*, pp. 60–61.

25. For some excellent analyses of the nature of authority in organizations see the following: Robert V. Presthus, "Authority in Organizations", *Public Administration Review*, 20 (Spring, 1960), pp. 86–91; Mertin J. Mandeville, "The Nature of Authority", *Journal of the Academy of Management*, 3 (August, 1960), pp. 107–118; Robert L. Peabody, "Perceptions of Organizational Authority: A Comparative Analysis", *Administrative Science Quarterly*, 6 (March, 1962), pp. 463–482; and Amitai Etzioni, "Authority Structure and Organizational Effectiveness", *Administrative Science Quarterly*, 4 (June, 1959), pp. 43–67.

26. "The Network of Authority", *Public Administration Review*, 18 (Winter, 1958), p. iii. Italics are Mr. Stahl's.

27. See below, pp. 141–142, for a description of this approach.

28. Mason Haire, "What Is Organized in an Organization?" in Mason Haire (ed.), *Organization Theory In Industrial Practice* (New York: John Wiley & Sons, 1962), p. 4. This whole chapter (pages 1–12 of the book) does a brief but effective job of exploding a number of organizational myths.

29. An authoritative National Industrial Conference Board report states: "The emphasis on principles as guides rather than dogma also stems from the fact that very few of them are stated in absolutes. The principle that 'everyone should report to only one boss' is one of the examples of an unequivocal directive." *Corporate Organization Structures*, by Harold Stieglitz, 1961 (Studies in Personnel Policy No. 183), p. 8.

30. Part of the problem in dealing with this principle is the semantic one of defining a "boss". Even by eliminating those who exercise authority or influence through informal means, and confining the definition to one who has the formal authority to (a) give orders, (b) assess and evaluate the work of subordinates, and (c) decide on promotions or merit increases, the principle is commonly violated.

31. See *Navy Management Review*, 8 (February, 1963), p. 3.

32. "Administration and the Conquest of Space", address before the National Conference of the American Society for Public Administration, Detroit, Michigan, Apr. 13, 1962, p. 9. See also on NASA's use of multiple bosses, Albert F. Siepert, "Administration of a Government Agency Under Conditions of Rapid Change", *Federal Accountant*, 12 (September, 1962), pp. 56–69.

33. Some enterprises, General Electric for example, do not believe in having either line or staff assistants and claim that they do not use them.

34. *New Patterns of Management* (New York: McGraw–Hill, 1961), pp. 104–115. Professor Likert's thesis is effectively stated in some detail in these pages and also in his booklet, *Developing Patterns of Management*, published by the American Management Association in 1956. See also Edgar H. Schein, "Forces Which Undermine Management Development", *California Management Review*, 5 (Summer, 1963), esp. pp. 31–33 for a lucid account of how specialized units impede the development and growth of managers.

35. *New Patterns of Management*, pp. 107–108.

36. "Innovation Challenges Conformity", *Harvard Business Review*, 40 (May–June, 1962), p. 72. Mr. Corson cites "The Art of Delegation" in *The Management Team*, Edward C. Bursk (ed.), (Cambridge: Harvard University Press, 1954), p. 6, for his authority on the reference to General Clay.

37. See, for example, Robert Tannenbaum and Warren H. Schmidt, "How To Choose a Leadership Pattern", *Harvard Business Review*, 36 (March–April, 1958), pp. 95–101, and Warren H. Schmidt, *The Leader Looks at the Leadership Dilemma* (Washington, D. C.: Leadership Resources, Inc., 1961).

38. See Ernest Dale, "Some Foundations of Organization Theory", *California Management Review*, 2 (Fall, 1959), pp. 71–84, for a plea to go beyond theorizing about universal principles into comparative research based on experience to find "intermediate guides that may be expected to work reasonably well in reasonably comparable circumstances . . . [by delineating] the area to which generalizations apply and the circumstances under which they hold true". See also Peter M. Blau, "The Comparative Study of Organizations", a paper prepared for delivery at the 1964 Annual Meeting of the American Political Science Association, Chicago, Sept. 9–12, 1964.

39. For an excellent account of the background, purposes, and methodology of this project see Frederick C. Mosher's unpublished paper, "Factors and Considerations in the Reorganization Process: A Research Program Based on Case Studies", prepared for delivery at the 1962 Annual Meeting of The American Political Science Association in Washington, D.C., Sept. 5–8, 1962.

40. The results of this project are expected to be published by Bobbs–Merrill in 1966 under the title: *Governmental Reorganization: A Case Book*. Professor Mosher reports as follows: "With regard to the principal variable under study in the project, the role of par-

ticipation, very little can be concluded at this stage. The single point of agreement among those involved in the project would appear to be that the initial hypothesis and its corollaries . . . were greatly over-simplified in relation to the complexity of data developed in the case studies".

41. For a discussion of some of the difficulties in empirical research see Edward C. Banfield, *op. cit.* Also see below, pp. 152–157.

42. For an interesting discussion of this point, see Harold J. Leavitt, "Unhuman Organizations", *Harvard Business Review*, 40 (July–August, 1962), p. 91.

43. See pp. 108–113.

44. Printed in House Document No. 460, 81st Congress, 2d Session, Feb. 1, 1950.

45. See also Gerald G. Fisch, "Line–Staff is Obsolete", *Harvard Business Review*, 39 (September–October, 1961), pp. 67–79.

46. For an excellent account of the relationships between central and divisional staff units, see Harold Stieglitz, "Staff–Staff Relationships", *Management Record*, 24 (February, 1962), pp. 2–13.

47. See, for example, his *Management By Results* (New York: McGraw–Hill, 1961), Chaps. 15, 16, and "Make Your Staff Pay Its Way", *Harvard Business Review*, 35 (March–April, 1957), pp. 115–122.

48. For a fuller discussion of this point, see pp. 48–50.

49. For examples, see Appendix B, Pars. IV, C and D.

50. "The Network of Authority", *Public Administration Review*, 18 (Winter, 1958), pp. iii, iv. Italics are Mr. Stahl's.

51. Lewis Carroll, *Through the Looking Glass*, Chap. 5.

52. For arguments against this categorical approach, see pp. 44–45.

53. "Centralization vs. Decentralization", *Advanced Management*, 20 (June, 1955), p. 12. This is the best single item on the whole problem of centralization and decentralization that I have seen.

54. For a description of these different types of organization see above, pp. 30–38.

55. For two excellent analyses of this problem see Daniel L. Kurshan, "Central Staff as a Control Agency", *Management Record*, 22 (April, 1960), pp. 9–14, and Harold Stieglitz, *op. cit.*

56. For a graphic illustration of what can happen when large-scale decentralization is attempted prematurely, see Richard J. Whalen, "The Unoriginal Ideas That Rebuilt Crown Cork", *Fortune*, 68 (October, 1962), pp. 119–123 ff.

57. The practical question may be whether the person with the

first-hand facts should communicate them upward to the person with broader perspective for decision, or whether the person with the broader perspective should communicate his information down to the person with the facts for decision.

58. One executive has said: "It is difficult to describe what this reorganization [involving further delegation of authority and fixing of responsibility for results] and its basic concept has wrought. I have facetiously compared it with the splitting of the atom in the amount of energy it has released. Never have I seen operating department heads so highly motivated, so determined, and so aggressive, or who work so hard to get outstanding results—both service and net revenue results." Matthias E. Lukens, "Practicing Management Theory", *Public Administration Review*, 18 (Summer, 1958), p. 226. For an overall view of the problem of motivation, see Harvey Sherman, "Improving Performance by Better Motivation of the Public Servant—United States Experience", paper delivered before the XI International Congress of Administrative Sciences, Wiesbaden, Germany, Aug. 29–Sept. 3, 1959.

59. General Motors was recently voted one of the ten best-managed companies in the United States, with a special citation for its organization, by the President's Panel of *Dun's Review*. Its outstanding organization has been attributed principally to the successful combination of the "freedom" and "nimbleness" of decentralization, with the "strategic power, over-all policies and economies" of centralization. See Thomas R. Brooks, "What Makes *GM* Go", *Dun's Review and Modern Industry*, 82 (September, 1963), pp. 30–32, 54–64.

60. See Chap. 5.

61. This was one of the four major trends in organization found in a recent study by the National Industrial Conference Board (*Corporate Organization Structures*, Studies in Personnel Policy, No. 183, 1961, Chap. 2). See also below, p. 127. A recent study of the ten best-managed companies in the United States found six common threads one of which was: "A truly decentralized corporate structure, as opposed to the lip service that passes for decentralization in so many companies". "What Makes a 'Best Managed Company' ", *Dun's Review and Modern Industry*, 82 (December, 1963), p. 41.

62. These categories were developed by W. H. Nesbitt, Director of Organization Planning, Westinghouse Electric Corporation, and are used here with his kind permission.

63. For an excellent discussion of some of the basic psychological factors affecting supervisor–subordinate relationships as they relate

to the problem of delegation, see Harry Levinson, "A Psychologist Looks at Executive Development", *Harvard Business Review*, 40 (September–October, 1962), pp. 69–75.

64. Harry Levinson has said: "The contemporary climate in American business and industry seems to be one in which mistakes are increasingly less tolerated or permitted". *Ibid.*, p. 71.

65. Inter-University Case Program, Case No. 9, revised (Indianapolis: Bobbs–Merrill, 1959), p. 1.

66. See, for example, Foundation for Research on Human Behavior, *Managing Major Change in Organizations* (Ann Arbor: The Foundation, 1961); Eli Ginsburg and Ewing W. Reilley, *Effecting Change in Large Organizations* (New York: Columbia University Press, 1957); Robert H. Guest, *Organizational Change: The Effect of Successful Leadership* (Homewood: Richard D. Irwin, 1962); and Paul R. Lawrence, *The Changing of Organizational Behavior Patterns* (Boston: Harvard University Press, 1958).

67. See below, pp. 108–113, for additional detail on certain other aspects of reorganizing.

68. See, for example, *The New York Times*, Nov. 18, 1962, p. 59.

69. See above, pp. 53–54.

70. See, for example, Lester Coch and John R. P. French, Jr., "Overcoming Resistance to Change", *Human Relations*, Vol. I, No. 4 (1948), pp. 512–532.

71. For a more detailed account, see Ginsburg and Reilley, *op. cit.*, Chaps. IV–VI.

72. On this subject, see Allen R. Janger, "Announcing an Organization Change", *Management Record*, 24 (October, 1962), pp. 8–11.

73. See below, pp. 136–143.

74. *Managing Major Change in Organizations*, 1961, pp. 55ff. See also Warren G. Bennis, "A New Role for the Behavioral Sciences: Effecting Organizational Change", *Administrative Science Quarterly*, 8 (September, 1963), pp. 125–165.

75. Some of the material in this chapter is adopted from a speech I delivered at the Fifth Annual Dean's Day Homecoming Conference, Graduate School of Business Administration, New York University, Feb. 15, 1958, on "Setting Objectives for Profits–Organization". This speech was published in the Proceedings of the Conference (New York University Business Series No. 34), pp. 66–69.

76. "Unhuman Organizations", *Harvard Business Review*, 40 (July–August, 1962), p. 97. See also C. Mansel Keene, "Administrative Reality: Advances, Not Solutions", *Public Administration Review*, 22 (September, 1962), pp 124–128.

77. "Unhuman Organizations", *Harvard Business Review*, 40 (July–August, 1962), p. 95.

78. *Dun's Review and Modern Industry*, 70 (December, 1957), pp. 40–42, 69–73.

79. Edward McCreary, "Countertrend to Decentralization: Top Management Tightens Control", pp. 32–34.

80. "Mirage of Profit Decentralization", *Harvard Business Review*, 40 (November–December, 1962), p. 140.

81. A. C. MacKinney, P. F. Wernimont, and W. O. Galitz, "Has Specialization Reduced Job Satisfaction?", *Personnel*, 39 (January–February, 1962), pp. 8–17.

82. *Ibid.*, p. 17.

83. Cf. Wilfred Brown, "A Critique of Some Current Ideas About Organization", *California Management Review*, 6 (Fall, 1963), pp. 3–12. Mr. Brown defends the concept of formal organization and attacks the emphasis given in recent years to informal organization.

84. "The Case for Benevolent Autocracy", *Harvard Business Review*, 36 (January–February, 1958), pp. 82–90.

85. *Harvard Business Review*, 35 (November–December, 1957), pp. 41–47.

86. See, for example, Martin L. Gross, *The Brain Watchers* (New York: Random House, 1962); Banesh Hoffman, the *Tyranny of Testing* (New York: Crowell–Collier and Macmillan, 1962); and William H. Whyte, Jr., *The Organization Man* (New York: Simon and Schuster, 1956), esp. Part IV and Appendix.

87. See, for example, Foundation for Research in Human Behavior, *Performance Appraisal and Review* (Ann Arbor: The Foundation, 1957); Philip R. Kelly, "Reappraisal of Appraisals", *Harvard Business Review*, 36 (May–June, 1958), pp. 59–68; and Douglas McGregor, "An Uneasy Look at Performance Appraisal", *Harvard Business Review*, 35 (May–June, 1957), pp. 89–94.

88. See above, pp. 89–96.

89. See above, pp. 53–54.

90. In another connection, Frederick C. Mosher has said: "The fact is that many sweeping reorganization proposals have resulted in greater rather than lesser expenditures, when they have affected them at all; yet almost all have been advertised and sold on the basis of economy". "Decision–Making in Defense: The Role of Organization—Old Concepts and New Problems", *Public Administration Review*, 18 (Summer, 1958), p. 173.

91. Based on a presentation made by Frederick C. Mosher at a panel session on "The Adminstration of Administrative Reorganiza-

tion" at the fifty–eighth annual meeting of the American Political Science Association, Washington, D. C., Sept. 7, 1962.

92. "Birth of an Organization: The Economic Cooperation Administration", *Public Administration Review*, 13 (Autumn, 1953), p. 236.

93. "The Politics of Administrative Organization: A Case History", *The Journal of Politics*, 19 (August, 1957), pp. 461–478.

94. *Ibid.*, p. 477.

95. For a good example, see "Decision–Making in Defense: The Role of Organization", a symposium in *Public Administration Review*, 18 (Summer, 1958), pp. 169–188.

96. David McCord Wright uses the term "the administrative fallacy" to refer to the common assumption "that when affairs are working without apparent friction and through proper channels, they are working well!" "The Administrative Fallacy", *Harvard Business Review*, 38 (July–August, 1960), p. 113. See also David W. Ewing, "Tension Can Be An Asset", *Harvard Business Review*, 42 (September–October, 1964), pp. 71–78.

97. For an excellent account of the systems approach to management, including discussion of its relationship to organization, see Seymour Tilles, "The Manager's Job: A Systems Approach", *Harvard Business Review*, 41 (January–February, 1963), pp. 73–81. See also Allan Harvey, "Systems Can *Too* Be Practical", *Business Horizons*, 7 (Summer, 1964), pp. 59–69.

98. Compare Charles E. Lindblom's concept of "successive limited comparisons" in "The Science of 'Muddling Through' ", *Public Administration Review*, 19 (Spring, 1959), pp. 79–88.

99. See The Port of New York Authority, *What's My Line?*, 1956.

100. For some of the most common myths about communications, see William H. Reed, "Communication in Organizations: Some Problems and Misconceptions", *Personnel Administration*, 26 (March–April, 1963), pp. 4–10.

101. Due to technological change and other reasons, some agencies and companies have, of course, disappeared or dwindled in size. But the overall trend toward larger single units is clear.

102. Figures for 1939 and 1949 are from *Business Week* (May 13, 1950), p. 102; 1960 figures are from *Fortune*, 67 (July, 1961), p. 168 and 67 (August, 1961), pp. 134, 136; 1964 figures are from *Fortune*, 71 (July, 1965), p. 150 and 71 (August, 1965), pp. 176, 178.

103. C. Northcote Parkinson, *Parkinson's Law* (Boston: Houghton Mifflin, 1957).

104. The "servicio" may be defined as a cooperative governmental unit set up within a ministry of the host government, with key operating positions filled by foreign technicians and local nationals, and with financial support provided by both the foreign and host governments, to carry out programs in such fields as agriculture, health, and education.

105. *Corporate Organization Structures* (Studies in Personnel Policy, No. 183), 1961, Chap. 2.

106. For support of my view see Herman M. Somers, "Organization—Door to Opportunity", *Civil Service Journal*, 3 (July–September, 1962), pp. 5–8, 15; Harlan Cleveland, "Dinosaurs and Personal Freedom", *Saturday Review*, 42 (Feb. 28, 1959), pp. 12–14, 38; Lyman W. Porter, "Where Is the Organization Man?", *Harvard Business Review*, 41 (November–December, 1963), pp. 53–61; and Leonard R. Sayles (ed.), *Individualism and Big Business* (New York: McGraw–Hill, 1963). See also Tannenbaum's thesis that the amount of power, authority, and influence available to all members of an enterprise is not a fixed total to be divided up between leaders and subordinates, but is subject to expansion or contraction for all. (Arnold S. Tannenbaum, "Control in Organizations: Individual Adjustment and Organizational Performance", *Administrative Science Quarterly*, 7 [September, 1962], pp. 236–257.) Also of interest is Bernard P. Indik, "Some Effects of Organization Size on Member Attitudes and Behavior", *Human Relations* (1963, No. 4), pp. 369–384.

107. For a brilliant analysis of this development, see Don K. Price, "The Scientific Establishment", *Science*, 136 (June 29, 1962), pp. 1099–1106. See also Don K. Price, "The Future of the Public Service", *Public Personnel Review*, 24 (April, 1963), pp. 83–87. For some interesting implications of "contracting out" by industry, see Sayles, *op. cit.*, pp. 27–33.

108. "How To Do Business With Governments", *Edison Electric Bulletin*, 30 (June–July, 1962), p. 220.

109. Letter from Thomas R. Reid to Harvey Sherman dated Nov. 29, 1963.

110. For an analysis of some of the management problems to be faced by the new instrumentality, see Beardsley Graham, "Satellite Communication", *International Science and Technology* (January, 1963), pp. 69ff.

111. National Industrial Conference Board, *The Economic Alamanac 1962* (New York: The Board, 1963), pp. 52–53. For a detailed analysis of the composition of the work force, past, present and future,

see U. S. Department of Labor, Bureau of Labor Statistics, *Occupational Outlook Handbook, 1966–67 Edition* (Washington, D. C.: Government Printing Office, 1966). Bulletin No. 1450.

112. Frederick Harbison, "Manpower and Innovation: Some Pointers for Management", *Personnel*, 36 (November–December, 1959), p. 8. The entire article (pp. 8–15) contains a cogent analysis of the implications for management of the emphasis on "brains" in the labor force.

113. Gertrude Deutsch, "Occupational Profile of the Factory Work Force, 1950–1960", *Business Record*, 20 (March, 1963), p. 18.

114. Ewan Clague, "Demographic Trends and Their Significance", in Hoke S. Simpson (ed.), *The Changing American Population*, a report of the Arden House Conference jointly sponsored by the Graduate School of Business, Columbia University, and the Institute of Life Insurance, 1962, p. 19.

115. Richard A. Johnson and Walter A. Hill, "Management's Dilemma—The Professional Employee", *California Management Review*, 5 (Spring, 1963), p. 38. The entire article (pp. 37–46) contains an excellent analysis of the needs and problems of the professional employee. See also, Jerome M. Rosow, "The Growing Role of Professional and Scientific Personnel", *Management Record*, 24 (February, 1962), pp. 19–33.

116. Ewan Clague, *op. cit.*, p. 14.

117. For an excellent analysis of the problem of organizing for scientific research, see Sherman Kingsbury, Lawrence W. Bass and Warren C. Lothrop, "Organizing for Research", in Carl Heyel (ed.), *Handbook of Industrial Research Management* (New York: Reinhold Publishing, 1959), pp. 65–91. See also Frederick Harbison, "Utilization and Development of High-Talent Manpower", *The Technology Review*, 60 (January, 1958), pp. 151–154, 170, 172, 174, 176, 178.

118. See especially C. P. Snow, *Science and Government* (Boston: Harvard University Press, 1961); Don K. Price *op. cit.*; Don K. Price, *Government and Science* (New York: New York University Press, 1954); James L. McCamy, *Science and Public Administration* (University: University of Alabama Press, 1960); William Kornhauser, *Scientists in Industry: Conflict and Accommodation* (Berkeley: University of California Press, 1962); Francis E. Rourke, "Bureaucracy in Conflict: Administrators and Professionals", *Ethics*, 70 (April, 1960), pp. 220–227; David E. Lilienthal, "Skeptical Look at 'Scientific Experts' ", *The New York Times Magazine*, Sept. 29, 1963, pp. 23, 79–80, 82, 84; Robert M. Hutchins *et al.*, *Science, Scientists and Politics* (Center for the Study of Democratic Institutions, 1963); Robert D. Best, "The

Scientific Mind *vs.* The Management Mind", *Industrial Research*, 5 (October, 1963), pp. 50–52; and Ralph M. Hower and Charles D. Orth (eds.), *Managers and Scientists* (Boston: Harvard Business School, 1963).

119. Ewan Clague, *op. cit.*, p. 17.

120. *Ibid.*, pp. 16–17.

121. See below, pp. 143–144.

122. "Implications of Technology for Management", in James R. Bright (ed.), *Technological Planning on the Corporate Level* (Cambridge: Harvard University Graduate School of Business Administration, 1912), p. 245. Italics are Mr. Henderson's. See also James R. Bright, "Opportunity & Threat in Technological Change", *Harvard Business Review*, 41 (November–December, 1963), pp. 76–86; and Max Ways, "The Era of Radical Change", *Fortune*, 70 (May, 1964), pp. 113–115, 210, 215–216.

123. *Managing Major Change in Organizations* (Ann Arbor: The Foundation, 1961), p. 1.

124. *Science and Public Administration* (University: University of Alabama Press, 1960), p. 76.

125. For an example of how one agency (the National Aeronautics and Space Administration) succeeded in doing this, see Albert F. Siepert, "Administration of a Government Agency Under Conditions of Rapid Change", *The Federal Accountant*, 11 (September, 1962), pp. 56–69. Along the same lines, see Jack B. Weiner, "The New Art of Free–Form Management", *Dun's Review*, 84 (December, 1964), pp. 30ff. See also Larry Cummings, "Organizational Climate for Creativity", *Academy of Management Journal*, 8 (September, 1965), pp. 220–227.

126. Sherman Kingsbury, "Arthur D. Little, Inc., A Small Society", unpublished paper, no date, p. 1.

127. Elting E. Morison, "A Case Study of Innovation", *Engineering and Science Monthly*, California Institute of Technology, 14 (April, 1950), pp. 10–11. Similar examples can be found in Edward H. Weiss, "The Pursuit of Creativity: The Paradox of Business", *Printers' Ink*, 283 (Apr. 19, 1963), pp. 49–51.

128. One astute observer sees an inherent paradox in the job of manager in that he has to accomplish both stability and change at the same time. See Leonard R. Sayles, "The Change Process in Organizations: An Applied Anthropology Analysis", *Human Organization*, 21 (Summer, 1962), pp. 62–67.

129. For a more detailed description of this approach see A. K. Wickesberg and T. C. Cronin, "Management by Task Force", *Har-*

vard Business Review, 40 (November–December, 1962), pp. 111–118; Auren Uris, "Balanced Talents Bring Team Success", *Nation's Business*, 50 (December, 1962), pp. 66–68, 70; and John M. Stewart, "Making Project Management Work", *Business Horizons*, 8 (Fall, 1965), pp. 54–70.

130. Kingsbury, *op. cit.*, pp. 3, 6.

131. For a more detailed account of this approach see Joseph A. Litterer, "Program Management: Organizing for Stability and Flexibility", *Personnel*, 40 (September–October, 1963), pp. 25–34; David I. Cleland, "Why Project Management?", *Business Horizons*, 7 (Winter, 1964), pp. 81–88; Paul O. Gaddis, "The Project Manager", *Harvard Business Review*, 37 (May–June, 1959), pp. 89–97; Allen R. Janger, "Anatomy of the Project Organization", *Business Management Record* (November, 1963), pp. 12–18; and National Industrial Conference Board, *The Product Manager System* (New York: The Board, 1965).

132. It has been estimated that over 700 U. S. companies now have formal planning units, with some 500 of them established within the last four years. "V. P. for the Future", *Time*, May 10, 1963, p. 89.

133. Richard C. Raymond, "Betting on New Technologies", in James R. Bright (ed.), *op. cit.*, p. 16. See also Bruce D. Henderson, "*Strategy* Planning", *Business Horizons*, 7 (Winter, 1964), pp. 21–24.

134. Murray D. Lincoln, *Vice President in Charge of Revolution* (New York: McGraw–Hill, 1960). Cf. Donald A. Schon, "Champions for Radical New Inventions", *Harvard Business Review*, 41 (March–April, 1963), pp. 77–86.

135. *Business Automation*, 12 (February, 1965), pp. 48–49. See also Francis Bello, "The War of the Computers", *Fortune*, 60 (October, 1959), pp. 128ff.; Robert L. Caleo, "What You Can Learn from the World's Largest User of EDP", *Administrative Management*, 23 (October, 1962), pp. 20–24; and Industrial Securities Committee of the Investment Bankers of America, "Computer's and Today's Business", *Management Review*, 52 (July, 1963), pp. 4–15.

136. U. S. House of Representatives, Committee on Post Office and Civil Service, *1964 Inventory of Automatic Data Processing (ADP) Equipment in the Federal Government*, July 1964, Committee Print, 88th Cong., Second Session, p. 9. See also, Lowell H. Hattery and others, "Electronic Data Processing in Public Administration, A Symposium", *Public Administration Review*, 22 (September, 1962), pp. 129–153.

137. *Harvard Business Review*, 36 (November–December, 1958), pp. 41–48. The two most comprehensive works on the overall problem

of the probable impact of automation and the computer on organization and management are Martin Greenberger (ed.), *Management and the Computer of the Future* (New York: John Wiley & Sons, 1962); and The American Assembly, *Automation and Technological Change*, John T. Dunlop (ed.), (New York: Prentice–Hall, 1962), especially Chap. 3 by Floyd C. Mann, "Psychological and Organizational Impacts", and Chap. 4 by Melvin Anshen, "Managerial Decisions".

138. For evidence to the contrary, see Hak Chong Lee, "On Information Technology and Organization Structure", *Academy of Management Journal*, 7 (September, 1964), pp. 204–210; "The Computer vs. Middle Management", *Personnel*, 43 (January, 1966), pp. 4–6; "A Boost for the Man in the Middle", *Business Week* (January 22, 1966), pp. 85–86, 89; and Donald R. Shaul, "What's Really Ahead for Middle Management?", *Personnel*, 41 (November–December, 1964), pp. 8–16.

139. *The New Science of Management Decision* (New York: Harper & Row, 1960), p. 38.

140. Somehow, the Leavitt–Whisler model reminds me of the caustic definition of the army that was current during World War II: "A System devised by geniuses for operation by idiots".

141. "Management As a Problem in Process Control", *Computers and Automation*, 11 (July, 1963), pp. 16–18, 20–21. See also his "Management in an Information-Automation Era", paper delivered at the XIII International Management Congress, New York, 1963, Paper No. CP6c.

142. Simon, *op. cit.*, p. 47. See also Ida Russakoff Hoos, "When the Computer Takes Over the Office", *Harvard Business Review*, 38 (July–August, 1960), pp. 102–112 for support of the view that the effect of the computer will be centralization of decision–making and downgrading of middle management.

143. "Information Technology and Decentralization", *Harvard Business Review*, 39 (November–December, 1961), p. 121. Italics are Mr. Burlingame's.

144. "Automation and the Coming Diffusion of Power in Industry", *Personnel*, 39 (May–June, 1962), p. 33.

145. "Organizational Implications of Automation", *Journal of the Academy of Management*, 3 (August, 1960), p. 123. See also Otis Lipstreu and Kenneth A. Reed, "A New Look at the Organizational Implications of Automation", *Journal of the Academy of Management*, 8 (March, 1965), pp. 24–31.

146. "Will New Methods of Data Processing Affect Organization

Planning?", results of a study by Herbert O. Brayer, *American Business*, 25 (November, 1955), pp. 9ff.

147. "The Impact of A.D.P. on Organization Structure", *O & M Bulletin*, 17 (August, 1962), pp. 124–132.

148. One of the most knowledgeable men I know in this field, Harold F. Smiddy, has said: "Throughout this paper statements are made questioning the assumption that today's massive, highspeed computer necessarily means radically altered organization structures for most businesses". ("Knowledge and Skills for Tomorrow's Business", unpublished paper prepared for the Centennial Symposium on Executive Development, Massachusetts Institute of Technology, Cambridge, Apr. 27–29, 1961, p. 27.) For a good example of a contrary (if somewhat mystical) view, see Bernard J. Muller–Thym, "The Real Meaning of Automation", *Management Review*, 52 (June, 1963), pp. 40–47. For some specific examples of how the introduction of electronic data processing has affected organization structure and behavior, see Allen I. Kraut, "How EDP is Affecting Workers and Organizations", *Personnel*, 39 (July–August, 1962), pp. 38–50; Floyd C. Mann and L. Richard Hoffman, "Individual and Organizational Correlates of Automation", *The Journal of Social Issues*, Vol. XII, No. 2, 1956, pp. 7–17; and Floyd C. Mann and Lawrence K. Williams, "Observations on the Dynamics of a Change to Electronic Data–Processing Equipment", *Administrative Science Quarterly*, 5 (September, 1960), pp. 217–256. Of course in certain specialized areas there may be a major impact. Thus, effective translation by computers may in the future significantly affect the division of work in groups engaged in this kind of work.

149. There is a story, probably apocryphal, that one company is so far advanced that letters of condolence to the families of employees who have died are composed and written by the computer!

150. John F. Burlingame, *op. cit.*, p. 123.

151. Louis Brownlow is reported to have said that the only sure solution for this problem is for the superior to come to work later than the subordinate! Apropos of the problem of the employee who comes to work late, the chief engineer of a major American company has said that in a study to determine whether there were any distinguishing characteristics between the creative and non-creative engineers of that company, the only one they could discover was that the creative engineers came to work late!

152. For a fascinating analysis of the question of whether metal brains will ever be able to do everything human brains can do, see Stanley Stark, "Creative Leadership: Human *vs.* Metal Brains", *Jour-

nal of the Academy of Management, 6 (June, 1963), pp. 160–169. See also, Gilbert Burck, "Will the Computer Outwit Man?", *Fortune*, 70 (October, 1964), pp. 120ff.

153. William J. J. Gordon has described the non–rational side of man as follows: "This 'rest of man' is the emotional, non–rational, the apparently irrelevant—the poetic. Yet it is this 'rest of man' which is so necessary for elegant solutions". "How To Get Your Imagination Off the Ground", *Think*, 29 (March, 1963), p. 1.

154. For some expressions of disenchantment with the role of the computer in Air Force decision–making, see Richard Witkin, "Air Force Aide Warns of Over–Automation in Military Decisions", *The New York Times*, Nov. 20, 1962, p. 19; and Francis X. Kane, "Security Is Too Important To Be Left To Computers", *Fortune*, 70 (April, 1964), pp. 146ff.

155. Edward H. Weiss, *op. cit.*, p. 50.

156. Murray A. Geisler and Wilbur A. Steger, "How To Plan for Management in New Systems", *Harvard Business Review*, 40 (September–October, 1962), pp. 103–110. For the theoretical application of a commonly used operations–research mathematical tool to a specific type of organization problem see Lawrence S. Hill, "The Application of Queuing Theory to the Span of Control", *Journal of the Academy of Management*, 6 (March, 1963), pp. 58–69.

157. See Joseph A. Litterer, "The Simulation of Organizational Behavior", *Journal of the Academy of Management*, 5 (April, 1962), pp. 24–35.

158. See W. R. Dill, William Hoffman, H. J. Leavitt, and Thomas O'Mara, "Experiences With a Complex Management Game", *California Management Review*, 4 (Spring, 1961), pp. 39–51.

159. See statement by Dr. J. K. Howard, former associate director, Organization Planning Department, U. S. Rubber Co., in *Personnel Administration*, 25 (July–August, 1962), pp. 63–64. A related development is the use of the human relations laboratory, or "sensitivity" training, as a tool for organizational analysis and change. For a case example, see Michael G. Blansfield, "Depth Analysis of Organizational Life", *California Management Review*, 5 (Winter, 1963), pp. 29–42.

160. For some of the limitations to the quantitative approach, see Homer Hoyt, "Schizophrenia in the Social Sciences", *Business Horizons*, 5 (Winter, 1962), pp. 95–99; Charles E. Lindblom, "The Science of Muddling Through", *Public Administration Review*, 19 (Spring, 1959), pp. 79–88; Raymond R. Mayer, "Scientific Management or Management Science?", *Advanced Management–Office Executive*, 2

(July, 1963), pp. 9–13, 29; Edward F. R. Hearle, "How Useful Are 'Scientific' Tools of Management?", *Public Administration Review*, 21 (Autumn, 1961), pp. 206–209; and David E. Lilienthal, *op. cit.*

161. "Administrative Reality: Advances, not Solutions", *Public Administration Review*, 22 (September, 1962), p. 127.

162. See George A. Shipman, "An Experimental Approach to Organization Design", *Public Administration Review*, 24 (September, 1964), pp. 194–195.

163. Mason Haire, "Introduction—Recurrent Themes and General Issues in Organization Theory", in Mason Haire (ed.), *Modern Organization Theory* (New York: John Wiley & Sons, 1959), p. 2. See also, Dwight Waldo, "Organization Theory: An Elephantine Problem", *Public Administration Review*, 21 (Autumn, 1961), pp. 210–225.

164. Haire, *op. cit.*, pp. 4–12.

165. See, for example, Herbert A. Simon, *Administrative Behavior*, 2d ed. (New York: Macmillan, 1957), and James G. March and Herbert A. Simon, *Organizations* (New York: John Wiley & Sons, 1958).

166. See, for example, *Personality and Organization* (New York: Harper & Row, 1957), and *Interpersonal Competence and Organizational Effectiveness* (Homewood: Richard D. Irwin, 1962). For a criticism of Argyris' approach, see Leonard R. Sayles, *op. cit.*, Chap. 8.

167. "Why Not Make Social Science Operational?", *Public Administration Review*, 22 (September, 1962), pp. 109–114.

168. An effective presentation of some of the reasons why practitioners "resist" the findings of researchers can be found in Joseph W. Newman's "Working With Behavioral Scientists", *Harvard Business Review*, 36 (July–August, 1958), pp. 67–74. For an analysis of how some of these resistances can be overcome, see Harold Guetzkow, "Conversion Barriers in Using the Social Sciences", *Administrative Science Quarterly*, 4 (June, 1959), pp. 68–81.

169. For an interesting presentation of some social science findings that are in direct conflict with each other, see Leonard R. Sayles, *op. cit.*, Appendix, pp. 185–195.

170. (New York: Harcourt, Brace & World, 1964), p. 12.

171. "A Fresh Approach to Administrative Analysis", *Public Administration Review*, 23 (September, 1963), p. 192.

172. "The Social Sciences and Management Practice", *California Management Review*, 6 (Summer, 1964), pp. 3–10.

173. See, for example, Fritz J. Roethlisberger and William J. Dickson, *Management and the Worker* (Boston: Harvard University

Press, 1939), and Henry A. Landsberger, *Hawthorne Revisited* (Itha-ca: Cornell University Press, 1958).

174. See, for example, Alfred J. Marrow, *Making Management Human* (New York: McGraw–Hill, 1957), and Lester Coch and John R. P. French, Jr., "Overcoming Resistance to Change", *Human Relations*, Vol. I No. 4 (1948), pp. 512–532.

175. See, for example, Rensis Likert, *New Patterns of Management* (New York: McGraw–Hill, 1961), and Universty of Michigan, Survey Research Center, *Productivity, Supervision and Employee Morale* (Human Relations Series 1, Report 1), 1949.

176. *The Changing of Organizational Behavior Patterns* (Boston: Harvard University Press, 1958).

177. *Organizational Change: The Effect of Successful Leadership* (Homewood: The Dorsey Press, and Richard D. Irwin, 1962).

178. See above, pp. 53, 108–109.

179. A major project involving the publication of a bi–monthly magazine and the production of special television programs has recently been initiated by Washington University in St. Louis to translate important social science research findings from the obscure language of the researchers into comprehensible English. (See *The New York Times*, July 25, 1963, p. 27.) For some of the reasons why jargon is used by social scientists, see George S. Odiorne, "Double Talk Cuts Egghead's Value to Business", *Nation's Business*, 51 (April, 1963), pp. 92–94.

180. For one interesting example of the type of research on this problem, see Winston Oberg, "Cross–Cultural Perspectives on Management Principles", *Journal of the Academy of Management*, 6 (June, 1963), pp. 129–143.

181. For a superb analysis of the overall problem of utilizing social science findings in practice, see "Can We Make Social Science Operational in Public Administration", a symposium containing articles by John M. Pfiffner, Merrill J. Collett, Thomas L. Gardner, and C. Mansel Keene, *Public Administration Review*, 22 (September, 1962), pp. 109–128. For some interesting examples of how social science findings could, and should, affect management and organization, see "Behavioral Science—What's In It For Management", *Business Management Record* (June, 1963), pp. 32–44. See also Marvin D. Dunnette and Bernard M. Bass, "Behavioral Scientists and Personnel Management", *Industrial Relations*, 2 (May, 1963), pp. 115–130.

182. See, for example, Lawrence L. Ferguson, "Social Scientists in the Plant", *Harvard Business Review*, 42 (May–June, 1964), pp. 133–143.

183. See, for example, John Perry, "Business—Next Target for Integration?", *Harvard Business Review*, 41 (March–April, 1963), pp. 104–115, and Charles E. Silberman, "The Businessman and the Negro", *Fortune*, 69 (September, 1963), pp. 97–99, 184, 186, 191–192, 194.

184. This is a paraphrase of the statement attributed to Frederick G. Donner, chairman of the board of General Motors that, "Business is, like war, essentially disorderly". Quoted in Thomas R. Brooks, "What Makes *GM* Go?", *Dun's Review and Modern Industry*, 82 (September, 1963), p. 30.

some noteworthy definitions
of organization

"Organization is a mechanism or structure that enables living things to work effectively together". Louis A. Allen, *Management and Organization* (New York: McGraw–Hill, 1958), p. 52.

"An organization is defined as a pattern of variables tending toward stability or equilibrium". Chris Argyris, "Understanding Human Behavior in Organizations: One Viewpoint" in *Moden Organization Theory*, ed. by Mason Haire (New York: John Wiley & Sons, 1959), p. 149.

"Of special importance is the concept of the organization as a small society, that is, a group of individuals welded together into a functioning team by certain devices, or bonds of organization". E. Wight Bakke, *Bonds of Organization: An Appraisal of Corporate Human Relations* (New York: Harper & Row, 1950), pp. 5–6.

"[Formal organization is a] system of consciously coordinated activities or forces of two or more persons". Chester I. Barnard, *The Functions of the Executive* (Cambridge: Harvard University Press, 1938), p. 73.

"What they [organizations] all have in common is that a number of men have become organized into a social unit—an organization—that has been established for the explicit purpose of achieving certain goals". Peter M. Blau and W. Richard Scott, *Formal Organizations: A Comparative Approach* (San Francisco: Chandler, 1962), p. 1.

"Organization planning is the process of defining and grouping the activities of the enterprise so that they may be most logically assigned and effectively executed". Ernest Dale, *Planning and Developing the*

Company Organization Structure (New York: American Management Association, 1952), p. 14 (Research Report No. 20).

"Organization is a means or a tool for achieving ends that can be gained only when a number of people work together. . . . 'Organization', as used by organization specialists, may be defined as a method of breaking down broad and overwhelming tasks into manageable and pinpointed responsibilities and at the same time ensuring coordination of the work". Ernest Dale, *The Great Organizers* (New York: McGraw–Hill, 1960), pp. v, 2.

"Organization is seen not as a chiseled entity, but as a shifting set of contained and ongoing counter phases of action. . . . The typical firm is thus a shifting set of contained disruptions, powered and guided by differentially skilled and committed persons". Melville Dalton, *Men Who Manage: Fusions of Feeling and Theory in Administration* (New York: John Wiley & Sons, 1959), pp. 4, 270.

"Organizations are social units oriented to the realization of specific goals . . . ." Amitai Etzione, *A Comparative Analysis of Complex Organizations* (New York: Free Press of Glencoe, 1961), p. 79.

"For the object of organization is control, or we might say that organization *is* control". Mary Parker Follett, "The Process of Control", in Luther Gulick and L. Urwick, *Papers on the Science of Administration* (New York: Institute of Public Administration, 1937), p. 161.

"Organization is the arrangement of personnel for facilitating the accomplishment of some agreed purpose through the allocation of functions and responsibilities". John M. Gaus, "A Theory of Organization in Public Administration", in John M. Gaus, Leonard D. White, and Marshall E. Dimock, *The Frontiers of Public Administration* (Chicago: University of Chicago Press, 1936), p. 66.

"The theory of organization, therefore, has to do with the structure of coordination imposed upon the work–division units of an enterprise". Luther Gulick, "Notes on the Theory of Organization", in Luther Gulick and L. Urwick, *Papers on the Science of Administration* (New York: Institute of Public Administration, 1937), p. 3.

"Formal organization—a pyramid structure of hierarchy, authority, functions, and rules. . . . Informal organization describes the groups within the plant, each group constituting, more or less, a social system". Sherman Krupp, *Pattern in Organization Analysis: A Critical Examination* (Philadelphia: Chilton, 1961), pp. 20–21, 29.

"In this study we shall be conceiving of a formal organization as a social system that is formed to serve certain purposes, and to which individuals and small groups act as contributors". Paul R. Lawrence, *The Changing of Organizational Behavior Patterns: A Case Study of*

Decentralization (Boston, Mass.: Harvard Business School, 1958), p. 6.

"The organization consists of a tightly knit, effectively functioning social system. This social system is made up of interlocking work groups with a high degree of group loyalty among the members and favorable attitudes and trust between superiors and subordinates. . . . Every organization is a human enterprise whose success depends upon the coordinated efforts of its members". Rensis Likert, *New Patterns of Management* (New York: McGraw–Hill, 1961), pp. 99, 178.

"The central principle of organization which derives from Theory X is that of direction and control through the exercise of authority. . . . The central principle which derives from Theory Y is that of integration: the creation of conditions such that the members of the organization can achieve their goals *best* by directing their efforts toward the success of the enterprise". Douglas McGregor, *The Human Side of Enterprise* (New York: McGraw–Hill, 1960), p. 49.

"Organizations are assemblages of interacting human beings and they are the largest assemblages in our society that have anything resembling a central coordinative system". James G. March and Herbert A. Simon, *Organizations* (New York: John Wiley & Sons, 1958), p. 4.

"Organization is the form of every human association for the attainment of a common purpose. . . . This term [coordination] expresses the principles of organization *in toto*; nothing less". James D. Mooney and Alan C. Reiley, *The Principles of Organization* (New York: Harper & Row, 1939), pp. 1, 5.

"Organization is the pattern of ways in which large numbers of people, too many to have intimate face-to-face contact with all others, and engaged in a complexity of tasks, relate themselves to each other in the conscious, systematic establishment and accomplishment of mutually agreed purposes". John M. Pfiffner and Frank P. Sherwood, *Administrative Organization* (Englewood Cliffs: Prentice–Hall, 1960), p. 30.

"By *formal organization* is meant the pattern of behaviors and relationships that is deliberately and legitimately planned for the members of an organization. . . . By *informal organization* is meant the whole pattern of actual behaviors—the way members of the organization really do behave—insofar as these actual behaviors do not coincide with the formal plan". Herbert A. Simon, Donald W. Smithburg, and Victor A. Thompson, *Public Administration* (New York: Alfred A. Knopf, 1950), pp. 85, 87.

"An oganization is a structure made up of positions and roles that people move in and out of without destroying the organization".

Victor A. Thompson, *Modern Organization* (New York: Alfred A. Knopf, 1961), p. 113.

"Organization . . . may be defined . . . as determining what activities are necessary to any purpose (or 'plan') and arranging them in groups which may be assigned to individuals". L. Urwick, *The Elements of Administration* (New York: Harper & Row, 1944), p. 36.

the organization of the port of new york authority

THE ORGANIZATION OF THE PORT AUTHORITY,
Office of the Executive Director, The Port of New York Authority,
PAI 10-1.00—February 21, 1962.

I. Introduction

A. Purposes

The purposes of this instruction are to describe the general plan of organization of the Port Authority, to define the authority and responsibilities of the line and staff departments and to prescribe some of the requisite conditions for their effective collaboration.

B. Relation to Other PAI's

This instruction is intended to serve as a general introduction to the "10 series" PAI's. PAI 10-1.01 is the current Port Authority Organization Chart. The remaining PAI's in this series describe the detailed functions, responsibilities, and relationships of the individual departments, divisions and offices.

C. Background

The current Port Authority organization structure grew out of a major reorganization that took place in the spring of 1952. This became necessary in order to deal effectively with the problems arising from the growth and diversification of the agency's activities. The organization structure best suited for operating a single type of transportation facility (tunnels and bridges) was no longer best suited for operating many types of facilities (addition of airports, marine terminals and land terminals), together with the Authority's other responsibilities under the Compact.

The most significant results of the reorganization were:

1. To establish four line departments: Aviation, Marine Terminals, Terminals, Tunnels and Bridges;

2. To locate in those departments the primary responsibility for assuring the overall success of the individual facilities and the requisite authority to achieve it. This is often referred to as "net revenue responsibility," but it embraces virtually all elements that determine successful management; it includes responsibility for the planning, operation, maintenance, and security of the facilities, negotiations with their tenants, the balancing of revenue considerations against public service obligations, and many related activities, all subject to:

a. Reliance on and full utilization of central staff departments possessing specialized skills needed for policy planning, advice, or technical service to the rest of the organization, with ready appeal by the staff departments to the Executive Director for resolution of issues that cannot be settled at the departmental level; and

b. Some limited controls by staff departments (subject to appeal to the Executive Director) in those cases where a staff department has been specifically delegated such functions by the Executive Director on behalf of the agency as a whole.

II. General Principles of Port Authority Organization

A. The Port Authority, in all of its activities, makes every effort to utilize or adapt the best practices of government and modern industry. Accordingly, many of the organizational principles observed in this agency are identical with those used in the best managed public agencies and private corporations. Briefly stated, some of the more important ones have to do with such fundamental practices as:

1. Carefully defining objectives for the organization and each of its sub–divisions

2. Delegating authority commensurate with responsibility

3. Grouping related tasks together in logical and systematic fashion

4. Pinpointing accountability for performance

5. Striking a sensible balance between having too many layers of supervision, on the one hand, and too many people reporting to any one supervisor, on the other

6. Maintaining clear lines of command but encouraging free and informal channels of communications

7. Emphasizing that organization has to do with people, depends upon human effort, and must satisfy human needs.

B. In addition to such basic concepts of good corporate management as the above, the Port Authority places strong emphasis on the following:

1. The form of organization, although important, is only one of the means by which the efforts of the entire staff are directed toward common goals; it is not an end in itself.

2. The organization structure and assignments of responsibility within that structure must change with time and circumstances. The Port Authority owes its existence and growth to the fact that swift changes in transportation patterns have forced the development of new methods of private and governmental action to cope with them. Change is to be expected, planned for, and welcomed.

3. The Authority is a unified organization. All parts contribute to the success of the whole enterprise and depend upon support from the other component parts of the organization. To the extent that conflicts and disagreements between organization units sharpen issues for decision at the next higher level and are reasonable expressions of differing ideas on how best to accomplish a common purpose, they are desirable; they are undesirable when they arise from personality conflicts, preoccupation with personal or jurisdictional status, confused allocation of responsibilities, or similar causes which tend to divide the staff and lead to antagonisms.

4. Problems of organization must be handled on a practical basis. The Authority is not bound by doctrinaire attitudes. Thus, some activities may be centralized or others decentralized, depending, in each case, on such factors as public convenience, economy, quality of service, availability of skilled personnel, need for control, and general effectiveness.

5. Every supervisor, including the Executive Director as well as a first–line supervisor, is responsible for achieving the most effective organization of the work of the people whom he supervises. He is also responsible for obtaining professional staff advice on such matters whenever appropriate. If such advice is available and he does not seek it out, he has failed in his responsibility.

6. The formal organization structure should be designed not only to achieve the most effective planning and execution of Port Authority functions, but should also contribute to high morale, personal development, and work satisfaction for the employees of the Port Authority.

III. The Role of the Line Departments

The directors of the line departments are held accountable by the Executive Director for the overall success of the facilities under their supervision. This entails responsibility, authority and accountability, subject to the provisions of Par. IV, for:

A. The net revenue position of their facilities. This includes control over expenses incurred by the facilities as well as the power, in some cases, to approve and, in other cases, to review or question expenditures charged to them by other departments or offices. It also includes control over the major elements which determine gross revenues—this covers the right of initiating leases, contracts and similar transactions concerning their facilities, as well as the right of prior review or approval of such transactions, if initiated by others;

B. The planning and initiating of proposals for modifying, enlarging or altering existing facilities under their jurisdiction and the right of prior review or approval of proposals, if initiated by others;

C. Participation in, and, as early in the process as is feasible, for control over the planning of the acquisition, construction or leasing of new or additional facilities, subject to certain overall limitations as to the comprehensive needs of the Port District;

D. The effective development, promotion, operation, maintenance, safety and security of, as well as the public service rendered by, their facilities.

IV. The Role of the Staff Departments

A. The directors of the staff departments are held accountable by the Executive Director for successfully:

    1. Assisting him in:

        a. Planning and developing future policies, programs, and projects;

        b. Establishing and maintaining standards of effective performance;

        c. Evaluating current and past operations in relation to these standards; and

        d. Modifying current and future programs accordingly.

    2. Administering and controlling certain Port Authority programs, as delineated in the PAI's or as assigned, on behalf of the Authority as a whole;

    3. Providing technical or specialized advice and assistance to the Executive Director, other departments, divisions, or facilities;

    4. Providing general administrative and other central services for the entire organization or special services to units whose workloads cannot individually support assignment of specialized personnel.

B. Staff departments partake, in varying degrees, of several or all of the elements described in Par. A. Thus, all staff departments, even those performing control or coordinating functions, have a common responsibility for giving service or advice to the other units of the Port Authority. Conversely, the common–service units frequently contain some element of advice, evaluation or control. Furthermore, depending on the subject matter, a staff department can either;

 1. Be the "responsible department," in the sense that it holds primary responsibility or authority for taking certain actions; or

 2. Serve in an advisory or collaborative capacity with other departments.

In the following paragraphs are furnished some guidelines to differentiate between these two types of situations.

C. Situations in Which Staff Departments Have Primary Responsibility

For specified purposes, such as those given below and many others, primary responsibility for certain activities is lodged in staff departments. In such cases, the individual PAI's spell out the limitations and conditions under which the staff department may exercise its authority.

 1. *Need to center more attention on policy considerations or on programs requiring special emphasis:*

 Examples:

 Assignment to Engineering Department of the responsibility for assuring the structural integrity of all buildings and other physical facilities constructed for the Authority;

 Allocation to Port Development Department of responsibility for initiating proposals for new construction or development projects to meet the objectives of the Compact and Comprehensive Plan and acting as the "Responsible Department" during the early planning phases;

 Establishment of a central unit under the Director of Finance to develop long range financial plans and to evaluate financial assumptions of proposed new projects (while the detailed economic analyses are prepared within the sponsoring departments).

 2. *Better executive and policy control:*

 Examples:

 Preparation and clearance of public statements by the Public Relations Department.

 3. *Greater uniformity, quality, or consistency of treatment:*

i.e., when the Executive Director has specifically lodged responsibility in a staff department in order to carry out a program requiring Authority–wide observance:

Examples:

Classification of jobs; methods of accounting for expenditures; administration of Suggestion System; police discipline; compulsory medical procedures; central purchasing.

4. *Better representation of the Port Authority:* i.e., where the Executive Director has designated a staff department to represent the interests of the Port Authority as a whole, in dealings with outside firms, agencies, or individuals:

Examples:

Public relations

Community relations

Financial relations

Port protection and promotion

Tenant relocation

5. *Greater economy:*

Examples:

Central payroll

Use of electronic computer

D. Situations in Which Staff Departments Have Advisory or Collaborative Responsibilities

Except for the type of functions described under IV C, all functions of staff departments are carried on for the purpose of advising or facilitating the work of the Executive Director, the line departments and all other parts of the organization. These functions are subject to continuous review and adjustment, depending on the subject matter. They are characterized by the considerable amount of give-and-take exchanged between the staff department and the other departments for whom or with whom it may be working at any particular time. Specific examples of such functions are:

Development and installation of standards of operation and maintenance—involves how the Operations Services Department works with the line departments

Use of consumer services space at public terminals—involves relations of the Real Estate Department with the line departments

Preparation of engineering designs calculated to result in Port Authority construction that will harmonize the objectives of economy, quality, efficiency, safety, aesthetics, and allied considerations—involves the Engineering Department's relations with the department sponsoring the project.

Planning of new construction or development projects—involves relations between the Port Development Department and the line departments, particularly in cases where the responsibility for a specific project has passed to the line department (the reverse of the situation described in Par. IV, C–1).

V. Interdepartmental Relationships

Underlying all formal assignments of authority are certain general principles that apply to all departments and to their dealings with each other:

A. The relationships among departments must be characterized by mutual trust and mutual respect for the contribution that each group can make to the solution of the common problem. One basic test of a department's sincerity in this respect is the extent to which it communicates with other departments—i.e., how well it keeps them informed of significant developments which directly or indirectly affect their work, the accuracy and timeliness of the information, and the courtesy, consideration and frankness with which their views are solicited.

B. Both the staff and the line departments should not place excessive emphasis on jurisdictional rights, but should undertake to obtain acceptance by persuasion, building informal relationships, performing high quality work within agreed time limits, and especially by demonstrating a realistic understanding of the problems and point of view of other departments. (This is commonly referred to as using the "authority of knowledge" rather than the "authority of rank.")

C. The line (as well as staff) should not become parochial, inflexible, or know-it-all; they should welcome new and fresh ideas, improvements in methods, and concern with long range needs.

D. Negotiations should be dominated by a sense of practicality, by a recognition of what makes sense in the situation and what will work, even when this collides with consistency, custom or precedent.

E. Negotiations should be characterized by informality, face-to-face contacts and good–humored attempts to resolve differences. But if a fundamental principle is involved and there is no other way, the issue must be thrashed out at higher levels and not allowed to fester inside the organization.

F. As a primary condition of organizational effectiveness, it must be taken for granted by all departments that the responsible department (whether line or staff) will adopt the recommendations of another department if they are sound and will reject them only for compelling reasons. If the other department is unable to persuade the responsible department, and a basic principle or policy issue is involved tying back to its own responsibility, the other department has the duty and responsibility of appealing the matter to the Executive Director.

G. When a department has made a recommendation or given advice which is not accepted or when its advice or concurrence should have been sought and was not, the department which rejected or ignored the advice, or failed to seek it, must answer to the Executive Director for any inadequacy of performance resulting from such decisions or such omissions.

H. When standards have been developed for Port Authority–wide application (more than one department) and have been incorporated in official statements of policy, such as the PAI Manual, or where the Executive Director has made it clear through other media or methods that certain standards are to be observed, the role of the staff department is no longer advisory but becomes one of inspection and reporting.

VI. Use of Central Services

In recent years there has been a trend toward giving each individual department, staff or line, some leeway with respect to the use of services and advice furnished by staff departments, thus:

A. To use or not to use many types of centralized staff activities, such as surveys, studies, consulting services, or the usual administrative or housekeeping services (e.g., duplicating, graphics, food services, etc.), provided that:

    1. The line and other staff departments will not build up competing or duplicating units, nor divert existing staff to such purposes, except in emergency, short–term situations.

B. When using centralized services, to come to a prior agreement with the staff department as to probable cost, duration, and scope of the services to be provided (the "chargeback" system).

C. To employ outside firms to furnish such services only when:

    1. It can be demonstrated that the outside firm has a special expertise that is not available in a staff unit or when it can be demonstrated that the outside firm can give equal or better service at substantially lower cost than the Port Authority staff unit; and

    2. By so doing, other Port Authority activities are not adversely affected; and

    3. There is no compelling reason of Port Authority policy or

public service which would dictate use of Port Authority staff.

VII. Accountability

Because of the inter–actions between line and staff departments, as well as among staff departments, the Port Authority management has been developing various methods to pinpoint accountability for performance. Some of the more significant ones are:

A. *The Net Revenue Concept.* This is the principal device that is used to hold line departments accountable for financial return on investment. However, since there are some situations in which the line department cannot fully control a decision, even when such decision may materially affect the department's revenue position, other methods are also needed to fix accountability for performance and results.

B. *Public Service Criteria*

1. Public Service at Port Authority Facilities:

The line departments are held accountable for furnishing to the public at large and to patrons of the facilities, in particular, high levels of safety, service, comfort and convenience. Indices of satisfaction or dissatisfaction are expressed through such media as (to name only a few):

Written and verbal statements from patrons and tenants

Written and verbal statements from representatives of state, local, or national governmental agencies or instrumentalities

Legislative proposals and enactments

Press coverage and editorial comment

Political speeches and platforms

Damage suits and tort claims

Since these public service factors cannot be subordinated to net revenues, the line department has a difficult and delicate job of balancing the two sets of considerations. The staff departments are expected to furnish to the line departments concerned relevant, adequate, and prompt information and advice on both matters (i.e., public service and net revenue) and are held accountable for failure to do so, as well as for failure to inform the Executive Director of major issues which have not been satisfactorily resolved with the line department.

2. Public Need for New or Expanded Transportation and Terminal Facilities or Services:

Several of the staff departments are held accountable for developing and advancing proposals for new or better facilities and services, when the overall needs of the Port District clearly justify them, even in cases where the revenue potential might be marginal. The line and other staff departments are accountable for giving such proposals earnest consideration and for providing information that will enable the Executive Director to evaluate the proposals fairly and realistically.

C. *Adequate and coordinated reporting.* Basic to all reporting are the financial reports. These show not only the revenue position of the various facilities, but also identify the expenditures incurred by each organization unit and show how these costs have been charged, prorated or allocated against each facility. In addition, the Authority places considerable emphasis on narrative reports (e.g., the bi–weekly reports to the Executive Director and the Executive Director's Weekly Report to the Commissioners). Other methods of reporting are developed for specific programs and for specific purposes (facility inspection reports, reports of maintenance workload, annual reports of progress on management improvement objectives).

D. *Performance standards.* Various types of standards are being and have been established for programs and activities of both line and staff departments, particularly in the fields of maintenance, cleaning, transcription and typing, personnel interviews, origin and destination studies, and financial and economic analysis. Other standards are being and will be developed, not only for programs that lend themselves to quantitative measurement, but also for those that involve considerable use of judgment, discretion and emphasis on quality. The program–type budget used by the Port Authority is an example of developmental work being done in this field.

One of the major benefits expected from this technique is that it should help the Executive Director and department heads to assess, more definitely and precisely than heretofore, accountability for successes, failures or partial failures, particularly in cases where the nature of the assignment requires joint effort by several different parts of the organization.

E. *The responsible department concept.* Another device that is used, when more than one department is involved in a problem or project, is to name a responsible department for the initial stages of a new project, with provision made for transferring this designation to another department, as and when certain predetermined conditions are attained. This type of situation is described in PAI 45–1.01.

F. *Limited use of committees.* A conscious effort is made to discourage the establishment of internal committees because they tend to diffuse accountability. Committees should generally meet the following tests before being authorized:

1. They should be set up for stated periods of time;

2. They should have a limited and specific objective which cannot readily be met by existing allocations of responsibility and authority;

3. The committees should have no decision–making powers and no operating responsibilities; they should be advisory to a specific line or staff official whose regular responsibilities encompass the type of work being done by the committee;

4. Continuing interdepartmental committees should be established by the Office of the Executive Director; and continuing committees within an individual department authorized by the office of the department director concerned;

5. Committees that are of a continuing nature should be periodically reviewed by the officials who originally established them in order to make sure there is a justifiable need for their continuance.

VIII. Responsibility for Organization Planning (see also Par. II, B–5)

Organization planning is the job of every supervisor. Specialized staff assistance and advice are available in this field, both from the Organization and Procedures Department and from outside management consulting firms, but all supervisors, at every level, are encouraged to:

A. Become thoroughly familiar with Port Authority management principles affecting organization;

B. Develop their own ideas as to the organization and functions of the groups whom they supervise and take the initiative for getting those ideas accepted and carried into effect;

C. Plan their future organization pattern: anticipate forthcoming changes in personnel, programs, methods or responsibilities; foresee the organizational implications of these changes; and have an organization plan ready or in mind, for use when the right time arrives.

mutable principles
of organization*

I. *Limitations of "Principles"*
    A. Principles fail as universal "rules of thumb" for organizing.
    B. "Rules" or "principles" can be of some value if the following limitations are recognized:
        1. Organization is effective only insofar as it helps the enterprise determine and achieve its short and long run goals.
        2. Organization is inevitably the result of a series of compromises which weigh a great number of possibilities about a specific or unique situation.
        3. Organization is a living, moving, fluid force.
        4. Organization does not exist in a vacuum; it is made up of people who react and respond to numerous different stimuli many of which escape precise definition or measurement.
        5. "Principles" may be mutually contradictory; the key is to know which one applies under what circumstances and to what extent.
    C. "Principles" should be regarded, therefore, as:
    "Considerations which, under normal circumstances, serve to develop questions which the organizer must answer in the light of the specific situation with which he is dealing".

---

* This paper was originally prepared by a group in the U.S. Bureau of the Budget under the direction of Harry H. Fite in 1945–46 for use in a series of training courses on organization and methods. I have taken the liberty of making a number of editorial and substantive changes from the original version.

D. Some of the major "principles" or "considerations" are listed below, followed in each case by some of the conditioning factors which must be weighed carefully in using them.

II. *The number of individuals reporting to one supervisor should not be more nor less than can be effectively coordinated and motivated.* ("Span of control" principle)

A. The smaller the span of control, the larger the number of levels between the top and bottom of an enterprise, and vice versa.

B. A small span of control tends to facilitate coordination and control; a large span of control tends to shorten lines of communication, motivate subordinates, encourage acceptance of responsibility and develop people.

C. The most effective span of control is *not* the same in every situation. Among the factors which must be considered in determining the optimum span of control for a given situation is the extent to which:

1. The work is routine and repetitive, or complex and diverse.

2. The work performed by different units or personnel is similar or dissimilar.

3. There is interaction among the units or personnel being supervised.

4. The employees are physically close to the supervisor.

5. The program is static or dynamic.

6. Policies and operations can be delegated.

7. There are standardized procedures in effect.

8. There is an effective control system in operation.

9. The supervisor is able to devote full time to operating his unit, or, correlatively, must spend time on non–managerial activities or on relationships with other people and units.

10. The supervisor is free from "fire fighting"—that is, solving spot problems.

11. The supervisor and his subordinates are of top caliber. (The "style of management" of the supervisor is important.)

12. There is a common bond of understanding within the work force acquired from training or experience.

13. The employees are accustomed to coordinating their efforts voluntarily.

14. The supervisor has help from line or staff assistants.

15. There is a desire or need to develop subordinates.

16. There is a desire or need to provide more time for the supervisor to spend on policy and planning matters.

D. Other important factors effecting the optimum span of control include:

1. The level of the hierarchy (top management, middle management or supervisory).

2. The state of technology (e.g., techniques of communications available).

III. *Unnecessary duplication and overlapping of functions should be avoided.*

A. Direct duplication, where a job is done in one place and the identical job is repeated elsewhere, is usually but not always wasteful.

B. Many cases of alleged duplication are of the type that are inevitable or desirable in any form of organization. For example:

1. Functions often are duplicated without involving doing the same work (e.g., central files and divisional files).

2. "Duplication" is sometimes a desirable device for bringing maximum force to bear on a problem (different specialists may be looking at the same problem from different points of view, or where more than one person interviews a potential job applicant).

3. Vertical "duplication" is involved to a certain extent whenever the work of an employee is subject to review from above.

4. Staff work may frequently be repeated at various levels of supervision.

5. Staff and line units working on the same problem (e.g., staffing) inevitably involve some degree of duplication.

6. Sometimes it is desirable to have different teams or individuals working on the same problem to insure creative ideas (e.g., on research projects).

IV. *Responsibility for a function should be matched by the authority necessary to perform that function.*

A. Much confusion in organizational thinking arises from the failure to recognize that there are nearly always some limitations on authority and responsibility:

1. An administrator may be considered to have full responsibility for a function although there are nearly always some limitations on his authority to carry it out:

a. A division chief may be held responsible for a program, although his authority may be limited by restrictions on his power to act in borderline cases, and by the usual administrative limits in personnel, finance, budget and office procedure fields.

b. Even when an administrator may have full authority to

act, he may still be subject to policy and practice requirements prescribed by his superiors.

2. On important or complex matters, authority and responsibility are almost always, in fact, shared rather than individual—both vertically and horizontally.

B. There are semantics problems with this principle, since "authority" has at least four meanings: (1) formal power to issue orders, (2) informal right of subordinate to accept or not accept orders, (3) authority inherent in the job, (4) authority of persuasion or knowledge. Moreover, responsibility is frequently confused with accountability.

V. *Authority and responsibility for action should "to the greatest extent possible" be decentralized to those actually performing the operations.*

A. Decentralization and centralization are relative rather than absolute terms.

B. There are many competing forces leading toward both centralization and decentralization. The result for any function in any particular enterprise must take into account all these forces.

C. Some of the more important considerations in determining the extent to which decentralization is desirable are:

1. Authority and responsibility for an activity cannot effectively be delegated until policies are spelled out so as to assure uniform administration.

2. Decisions should ordinarily be made at the level with adequate competence, information, skills and perspective.

3. Certain matters (requests from important figures, etc.) take on top–side importance because of the potential repercussions if the case is mishandled.

4. The importance or size of an item may have a bearing on the extent to which performance can be delegated (e.g., an agency head may feel it necessary to approve personally all projects costing over $50,000.)

5. It may be feasible to decentralize certain activities to operating divisions, but in the interest of efficiency, economy or consistency they should be centralized.

6. If an activity is located in another city, there is more reason to decentralize the activity than if it is located nearby.

7. If immediate or instantaneous decisions are needed, there is more reason for decentralizing authority to the "grass roots".

8. An activity cannot be delegated if there are not trained and capable subordinates to carry out the responsibilities.

9. Certain "reserved" or "executive" powers are rarely subject to delegation:

    a. Program planning.

    b. Coordinating.

    c. Evaluating.

    d. Developing subordinates.

VI. *No member of an organization should be accountable to more than one supervisor.*

A. Where there is a deputy or assistant in the "line of command", a subordinate will usually in fact be reporting to two superiors.

B. Where organization is on a project basis, a subordinate may be assigned to projects with different project leaders.

C. Staff units, although theoretically operating in the name of their chief, may in fact be issuing orders to or exercising controls over subordinates who do not "report to" them.

D. Informal leaders within a group may frequently exercise control and on some matters may be "obeyed" as though they were the formal supervisor.

VII. *Throughout the organization, each member should know to whom he reports and who reports to him.*

A. A clear understanding of the lines of command and accountability is useful. (But see qualifications under Principle No. VI.)

B. However, it is important to recognize that

    1. Interrelationships exist outside of the line of command that require reporting to and working with many other people for effective work.

    2. The line of command should not be the only line of communication for effective teamwork.

VIII. *Every necessary function of an organization should be assigned to a unit of that organization.*

A. There are advantages in making sure that somebody is clearly responsible for doing every job that has to be performed to fulfill objectives and programs.

B. This must be qualified by the fact that some responsibilities must be shared among various units. For example,

    1. Organization means division of work in one of several alternative ways. This means a common responsibility among several units for assuring the fulfillment of overall goals.

    2. Planning is the joint responsibility of everybody in an organization.

    3. Customer good–will is the responsibility of the manufacturing division in producing a satisfactory product, of the supply divi-

sion in getting merchandise delivered as promised, of the sales division in honestly representing the product, etc.

4. Staff and line units share responsibility for such objectives as effective personnel administration, good public relations, efficient procedures, etc.

IX. *The responsibilities assigned to each unit should be clear cut.*

A. Vague assignments of responsibility encourage confusion, recrimination, and jurisdictional conflict.

B. On the other hand,

1. Too specific definitions of responsibility leave the way open for not doing things because they were not specifically defined.

2. Broad definintions of responsibility encourage initiative, resourcefulness and teamwork.

3. New areas of activity often can be handled better by deferring detailed definition of responsibilities until there is sufficient experience with the new activity.

X. *Uniform methods and procedures should be installed when necessary or desirable for efficiency, economy or consistency.*

A. Standardization should be approached with caution to make certain that the "one best way" is really best in all circumstances.

B. The main factors to consider are:

1. Variations between divisions and regions as to

a. Training and experience of personnel.

b. Local customs or conditions such as climate, economic factors.

c. The nature of the problems and work.

d. Volume of work.

2. Stability, maturity, and other features of a program that make it particularly fertile for standardizing on the "one best way".

3. Individual differences and motivations.

4. Need for creativity and experimentation.

bibliography

A. GENERAL

Allen, Louis A. *Management & Organization*. New York: McGraw-Hill, 1958.

Argyris, Chris. *Integrating the Individual and the Organization*. New York: John Wiley & Sons, 1964.

Argyris, Chris. *Interpersonal Competence and Organizational Effectiveness*. Homewood: Richard D. Irwin, 1962.

Argyris, Chris. *Personality and Organization*. New York: Harper & Row, 1957.

Argyris, Chris. *Understanding Organizational Behavior*. Homewood: Dorsey Press, 1960.

Bakke, E. Wight. *Bonds of Organization*. New York: Harper & Row, 1950.

Barnard, Chester I. *The Functions of the Executive*. Cambridge: Harvard University Press, 1938.

Barnard, Chester I. *Organization and Management*. Cambridge: Harvard University Press, 1948.

Blau, Peter M. and W. Richard Scott. *Formal Organizations, A Comparative Approach*. San Francisco: Chandler, 1962.

Caplow, Theodore. *Principles of Organization*. New York: Harcourt, Brace & World, 1964.

Carzo, Rocco Jr. "Organizational Realities", *Business Horizons*, 4 (Spring, 1961), pp. 95–104.

Chandler, Alfred D. *Strategy and Structure*. Cambridge: The Massachusetts Institute of Technology Press, 1962.

Chapple, Eliot D. and Leonard R. Sayles. *The Measure of Manage-

ment; Designing Organization for Human Effectiveness. New York: Macmillan, 1961.

Cooper, William W. and others. (eds.). *New Perspectives in Organization Research.* New York: John Wiley & Sons, 1964.

Dale, Ernest. *Planning and Developing the Company Organization Structure.* New York: American Management Association, 1952. (Research Report No. 20).

Dale, Ernest. "Some Foundations of Organization Theory", *California Management Review,* 2 (Fall, 1959), pp. 71–84.

Dale, Ernest. *The Great Organizers.* New York: McGraw–Hill, 1960.

Dalton, Melville. *Men Who Manage.* New York: John Wiley & Sons, 1959.

Etzioni, Amitai. *A Comparative Analysis of Complex Organizations.* New York: Free Press of Glencoe, 1961.

Etzioni, Amitai. *Complex Organizations; A Sociological Reader.* New York: Holt, Rinehart & Winston, 1961.

Etzioni, Amitai. *Modern Organizations.* New York: Prentice–Hall, 1964.

Fisch, Gerald G. *Organization for Profit.* New York: McGraw–Hill, 1964.

Golembiewski, Robert T. *Behavior and Organization; O & M and the Small Group.* Chicago: Rand McNally & Co., 1962.

Guest, Robert H. "Job Enlargement—A Revolution in Job Design", *Personnel Administration* (March, 1957), pp. 9–16.

Gulick, Luther. "Notes on the Theory of Organization", in Luther Gulick and L. Urwick. (eds.). *Papers on the Science of Administration.* New York: Institute of Public Administration, 1937.

Haire, Mason. (ed.). *Modern Organization Theory: A Symposium.* New York: John Wiley & Sons, 1959.

Haire, Mason. (ed.). *Organization Theory in Industrial Practice.* New York: John Wiley & Sons, 1962.

Kahn, Robert L. and Elise Boulding. (eds.). *Power and Conflict in Organizations.* New York: Basic Books, 1964.

Kaufman, Herbert. "Why Organizations Behave As They Do; An Outline of a Theory", Papers Presented at an Interdisciplinary Seminar on Administrative Theory, University of Texas, March 20–21, 1961.

Krupp, Sherman. *Pattern in Organizational Analysis; A Critical Examination.* Philadelphia: Chilton Co., 1961.

Lawrence, Paul R. and others. *Organizational Behavior and Administration: Cases, Concepts and Research Findings.* Homewood: Richard D. Irwin, 1961.

Leavitt, Harold J. (ed.). *The Social Science of Organizations: Four Perspectives.* Englewood Cliffs: Prentice–Hall, 1963.

Leavitt, Harold J. "Unhuman Organizations", *Harvard Business Review*, 40 (July–August, 1962), pp. 90–98.

Lepawsky, Albert. *Administration; The Art and Science of Organization and Management.* New York: Alfred A. Knopf, 1949.

Likert, Rensis. *New Patterns of Management.* New York: McGraw–Hill, 1961.

Litterer, Joseph A. *The Analysis of Organizations.* New York: John Wiley & Sons, 1965.

Litterer, Joseph A. (ed.). *Organizations: Structure and Behavior.* New York: John Wiley & Sons, 1963.

March, James G. (ed.). *Handbook of Organizations.* Chicago: Rand McNally & Co., 1965.

March, James G. and Herbert A. Simon. *Organizations.* New York: John Wiley & Sons, 1958.

McGregor, Douglas. *The Human Side of Enterprise.* New York: McGraw–Hill, 1960.

Mooney, James D. *The Principles of Organization.* New York: Harper & Row, 1947.

National Industrial Conference Board. *Charting the Company Organization Structure.* New York: National Industrial Conference Board, 1959.

National Industrial Conference Board. *Corporate Organization Structures.* New York: National Industrial Conference Board, 1961.

Pfiffner, John M. and Frank P. Sherwood. *Administrative Organization.* Englewood Cliffs: Prentice–Hall, 1960.

Presthus, Robert. *The Organizational Society.* New York: Alfred A. Knopf, 1962.

Rubenstein, Albert H. and Chadwick J. Haberstrok. (eds.). *Some Theories of Organization.* Homewood: Richard D. Irwin, 1960.

Salveson, Melvin E. *Dynamic Organization Planning.* New Canaan: Center for Advanced Management, 1959.

Sayles, Leonard. *Managerial Behavior.* New York: McGraw–Hill, 1964.

Scott, William G. "Organization Theory; An Overview and Appraisal", *Journal of the Academy of Management*, 4 (April, 1961), pp. 7–26.

Selznick, Philip. "Foundations of the Theory of Organization", *American Sociological Review*, 13 (February, 1948), pp. 25–35.

Simon, Herbert A. *Administrative Behavior.* 2d ed. New York: Macmillan, 1957.

Simon, Herbert A. "On the Concept of Organizational Goal", *Administrative Science Quarterly*, 9 (June, 1964), pp. 1–22.

Simon, Herbert A. "Proverbs of Administration", *Public Administration Review*, 6 (Winter, 1946), pp. 53–67.

Simon, Herbert A., Donald W. Smithburg, and Victor A. Thompson. *Public Administration*. New York: Alfred A. Knopf, 1950.

Stieglitz, Harold. "Developing Patterns in Organization Structures", *Management Record*, 23 (July–August, 1961), pp. 2–7.

Stieglitz, Harold. "Organization of the Chief Executive's Job", *Management Record*, 23 (February, 1961), pp. 2–9.

Tannenbaum, Robert, Irving R. Weschler, and Fred Massarik. *Leadership and Organization; A Behavioral Approach*. New York: McGraw–Hill, 1961.

Thompson, Victor A. *Modern Organization*. New York: Alfred A. Knopf, 1961.

Urwick, L. "Organization as a Technical Problem", in Luther Gulick and L. Urwick, (eds.). *Papers on the Science of Administration*. New York: Institute of Public Administration, 1937.

Waldo, Dwight. "Organizational Theory: An Elephantine Problem", *Public Administration Review*, 21 (Autumn, 1961), pp. 210–225.

Whyte, William Foote. *Man and Organization: Three Problems in Human Relations in Industry*. Homewood: Richard D. Irwin, 1959.

Woodward, Joan. *Industrial Organization: Theory and Practice*. London: Oxford University Press, 1965.

Worthy, James C. "Organization Structure and Employee Morale", *American Sociological Review*, 15 (April, 1950), pp. 169–179.

B. AUTHORITY IN ORGANIZATION

Brown, David S. *The Leader Looks at Authority and Hierarchy*. Washington, D.C.: Leadership Resources, 1961.

Etzioni, Amitai. "Authority Structure and Organizational Effectiveness", *Administrative Science Quarterly*, 4 (June, 1959), pp. 43–67.

Mandeville, Mertin J. "The Nature of Authority", *Journal of the Academy of Management*, 3 (August, 1960), pp. 107–118.

Peabody, Robert L. *Organizational Authority*. New York: Atherton Press, 1964.

Presthus, Robert V. "Authority in Organizations", *Public Administration Review*, 20 (Spring, 1960), pp. 86–91.

Trickett, Joseph M. "An Integrated Concept of Authority", *Management Record*, 24 (May, 1962), pp. 19–22.

C. Centralization / Decentralization

Bibby, Dause L., V. H. Viot, and Ernest Dale. "Decentralization—How Much and When?", *Advanced Management*, 24 (January, 1959), pp. 14–20.

Cleaveland, Frederic N. "Administrative Decentralization in the U.S. Bureau of Reclamation", *Public Administration Review*, 13 (Winter, 1953), pp. 17–29.

Dale, Ernest. "Centralization vs. Decentralization", *Advanced Management*, 20 (June, 1955), pp. 11–16.

Dearden, John. "Mirage of Profit Decentralization", *Harvard Business Review*, 40 (November–December, 1962), pp. 140–154.

Efferson, Carlos A. "Relationship Between Corporate and Divisional Staff", *Management Record*, 24 (May, 1962), pp. 23–27.

Kline, Bennett E. and Norman H. Martin. "Freedom, Authority and Decentralization", *Harvard Business Review*, 36 (May–June, 1958), pp. 69–75.

Simon, Herbert A. and others. *Centralization vs. Decentralization in Organizing the Controller's Department*. New York: Controllership Foundation, 1954.

Stieglitz, Harold. "Staff-Staff Relationships", *Management Record*, 24 (February, 1962), pp. 2–13.

D. Delegation

Corson, John J. "How To Delegate Responsibility", *Nation's Business* (May, 1956), pp. 84–88.

Gardner, Neely D. and John N. Davis. *The Art of Delegating*. Garden City: Doubleday & Co., 1965.

Laird, Donald and Eleanor Laird. *The Techniques of Delegating—How To Get Things Done Through Others*. New York: McGraw-Hill, 1957.

Levinson, Harry. "A Psychologist Looks at Executive Development", *Harvard Business Review*, 40 (September–October, 1962), pp. 69–75.

Newman, William H. "Overcoming Obstacles to Effective Delegation", *The Management Review*, 45 (January, 1956), pp. 36–41.

E. Impact of Automation and the Computer on Organization

American Assembly, *Automation and Technological Change*, ed. by John T. Dunlop. Englewood Cliffs: Prentice–Hall, 1962.

Burck, Gilbert. *The Computer Age, and Its Potential for Management*. New York: Harper & Row, 1965.

Burlingame, John F. "Information Technology and Decentralization", *Harvard Business Review*, 39 (November–December, 1961), pp. 121–126.

"Electronic Data Processing in Public Administration; a Symposium", *Public Administration Review*, 22 (September, 1962), pp. 129–152.

Greenberger, Martin. (ed.). *Management and the Computer of the Future.* New York: John Wiley & Sons, 1962.

Hoos, Ida Russakoff. "When The Computer Takes Over The Office", *Harvard Business Review*, 38 (July–August, 1960), pp. 102–112.

Kraut, Allen I. "How EDP is Affecting Workers and Organizations", *Personnel*, 39 (July–August, 1962), pp. 38–50.

Leavitt, Harold J. and Thomas L. Whisler. "Management in the 1980's", *Harvard Business Review*, 36 (November–December, 1958), pp. 41–48.

Lee, Hak Chong. *The Impact of Electronic Data Processing Upon the Patterns of Business Organization and Administration.* Albany: State University of New York, 1965.

Lipstreu, Otis. "Organizational Implications of Automation", *Journal of the Academy of Management*, 3 (August, 1960), pp. 119–124.

Raffaele, Joseph A. "Automation and the Coming Diffusion of Power in Industry", *Personnel*, 39 (May–June, 1962), pp. 29–39.

Schultz, George P. and Thomas L. Whisler. (eds.). *Management Organization and the Computer.* New York: Free Press of Glencoe, 1960.

Shaul, Donald R. "What's Really Ahead for Middle Management?", *Personnel*, 41 (November–December, 1964), pp. 8–16.

Simon, Herbert A. *The New Science of Management Decision.* New York: Harper & Row, Publishers, 1960.

"The Impact of A.D.P. on Organization Structure", *O & M Bulletin*, 17 (August, 1962), pp. 127–132.

"Will New Methods of Data Processing Affect Organization Planning?", results of a study by Herbert O. Brayer, *American Business*, 25 (November, 1955), pp. 9–11ff.

F. ORGANIZATIONAL CHANGE

Bennett, Thomas R. II. *The Leader Looks at the Process of Change.* Washington, D.C.: Leadership Resources, 1961.

Bennis, Warren G. "A New Role for the Behavioral Sciences: Effecting Organizational Change", *Administrative Science Quarterly*, 8 (September, 1963), pp. 125–165.

Bennis, Warren G., Kenneth D. Benne, and Robert Chin. (eds.). *The Planning of Change*. New York: Holt, Rinehart & Winston, 1961.

Cooper, Joseph D. "Organizations: Is This Change Necessary?", *Management Review*, 51 (December, 1962), pp. 4–10.

"Decision Making in Defense: The Role of Organization", *Public Administration Review*, 18 (Summer 1958), pp. 169–188.

Foundation for Research on Human Behavior. *Managing Major Change in Organizations*. Ann Arbor: Foundation for Research on Human Behavior, 1961.

Ginzberg, Eli and Ewing W. Reilley. *Effecting Change in Large Organizations*. New York: Columbia University Press, 1957.

Guest, Robert H. *Organizational Change: The Effect of Successful Leadership*. Homewood: Richard D. Irwin, 1962.

Janger, Allen R. "Announcing an Organization Change", *Management Record*, 24 (October, 1962), pp. 8–11.

Kaufman, Herbert. *The New York City Health Centers*. Indianapolis: Bobbs-Merrill, 1959 (Inter-University Case Program # 9).

Lawrence, Paul R. *The Changing of Organizational Behavior Patterns*. Boston: Harvard Business School, 1958.

Lippit, Ronald, Jeanne Watson, and Bruce Westley. *The Dynamics of Planned Change*. New York: Harcourt, Brace & Co., 1958.

Mosher, Frederick C. "Factors and Considerations in the Reorganization Process: A Research Program Based on Case Studies", a paper prepared for delivery at the 1962 Annual Meeting of the American Political Science Association in Washington, D.C., September 5–18, 1962.

Mosher, Frederick C. "Some Notes on Reorganization in Public Agencies", in Roscoe C. Martin. (ed.). *Public Administration and Democracy*. Syracuse: Syracuse University Press, 1965.

Penniman, Clara. "Reorganization and the Internal Revenue Service", *Public Administration Review*, 21 (Summer, 1961), pp. 121–130.

Rourke, Francis E. "The Politics of Administrative Organization: A Case History", *Journal of Politics*, 19 (August, 1957), pp. 461–478.

Sayles, Leonard R. "The Change Process in Organizations: An Applied Anthropology Analysis", *Human Organization*, 21 (Summer, 1962), pp. 62–67.

G.   STAFF–LINE RELATIONSHIPS

American Management Association. *Line–Staff Relationships in Production*. New York: American Management Association, 1957.

Dale, Ernest and Lyndall F. Urwick. *Staff in Organization*. New York: McGraw–Hill, 1960.

Dalton, Melville. "Conflicts Between Staff and Line Managerial Officers", *American Sociological Review*, 15 (June, 1950), pp. 342–351.

Fisch, Gerald G. "Line-Staff is Obsolete", *Harvard Business Review*, 39 (September–October, 1961), pp. 67–79.

Golembiewski, Robert T. "Toward the New Organization Theories: Some Notes on 'Staff' ", *Midwest Journal of Political Science*, 5 (August, 1961), pp. 237–259.

Juran, J. M. "Improving the Relationship Between Staff and Line —An Assist from the Anthropologists", *Personnel*, 32 (May, 1956), pp. 515–524.

Kurshan, Daniel L. "Central Staff as a Control Agency", *Management Record*, 22 (April, 1960), pp. 9–14.

National Industrial Conference Board. *Improving Staff and Line Relationships*. New York: National Industrial Conference Board, 1956. (Studies in Personnel Policy No. 153).

Pollock, Ross. *The Leader Looks at Staff-Line Relationships*. Washington, D.C.: Leadership Resources, 1961.

Rourke, Francis E. "Bureaucracy in Conflict: Administrators and Professionals", *Ethics*, 70 (April, 1960), pp. 220–227.

Sampson, R. C. *The Staff Role in Management*. New York: Harper & Row, 1955.

Schleh, Edward C. "Make Your Staff Pay Its Way", *Harvard Business Review*, 35 (March–April, 1957), pp. 115–122.

Stahl, O. Glenn. "The Network of Authority", *Public Administration Review*, 18 (Winter, 1958), pp. ii–iv; "More on the Network of Authority", *Public Administration Review*, 20 (Winter, 1960), pp. 35–37.

Stene, Edwin O. "Seven Letters: A Case in Public Management", *Public Administration Review*, 17 (Spring, 1957), pp. 83–90.

Toussaint, Maynard N. "Line-Staff Conflict: Its Causes and Cure", *Personnel*, 39 (May–June, 1962), pp. 8–20.

index

N.B. References are to page numbers (e.g., "30" = page 30), or to notes (e.g., "n137" = note 137, beginning on page 174 in the Notes, pages 161 through 180), or to Appendices A, B, or C (indicated as ApA, ApB, and ApC, respectively).